Roundabout:
Orpington's Little Buses

Tom Gurney

Red Bus Publishing

This Edition: August 2010

ROUNDABOUT:
Orpington's Little Buses

ISBN: 978-0-9566131-0-3

Published by: Red Bus Publishing, Orpington, Kent.

Printed by: Catford Print Centre, London SE6

Copyright: Red Bus Publishing / Tom Gurney 2010

Acknowledgements: the author gratefully acknowledges the kind assistance, anecdotes, photographs and other information supplied by many individuals during his research into creating this publication, but in particular thanks to Paul Bishop, Austin Blackburn, Martin Clitheroe, Bryan Constable, Richard Cains, E.L. Collinson, Bernie Costello, Brian Champion, James Fullick, Karl Gurney, David Hales, Gwen & Robbie Hood, David Hulls, Andrew Jeffreys, Adrian Jones, Richard Lancaster, Peter Larking, John Parkin, Julian Smith, Chris Suggitt, Graham Walker, Brian Wharf, Wai Wong, and Gary Wood.

Paul Bishop has devised an excellent website dedicated to the Roundabout story:

www.roundabout.moonfruit.com

Front Cover: "THE TIP TOP LOAF": MRL67 *"Blackbird II"* on route R11 in Cray Avenue passing the famous loaf of bread and cheery scrolled "Tip Top" bakery sign.

Photo by K. Gurney

Frontispiece: "THE CLIMB": OV3 *"Tornado"* makes good use of her unique 4-speed gearbox to fly up Poverest Road on route R3 to Petts Wood.   *Photo by K. Gurney*

Rear Cover Upper: "THE COFFEE BREAK": RH8 *'Swan'* on route R2 rests briefly at the Melody Road stand, Biggin Hill Valley, with her driver enjoying a nice refreshing cuppa between trips.   *Photo by Tom Gurney*

Rear Cover Lower: "THE ROBIN HOOD RACER": The RH fleet was built alongside machines designed for speed on water rather than land! Brian Champion of Robin Hood Racing was Robbie Hood's company photographer and renowned speedboat racing team driver. Robbie and Brian together raced in and won the 1984 World Off-shore Powerboat Championships for class 3C [single engine] and 3D [twin engine]. RH1 'Kestrel' shows off her fresh paint quality for a final photo call, as the first Roundabout bus departs the marine yard on trade plates bound for Selkent HQ. *Photo: courtesy Brian Champion / Robbie Hood*

2

CONTENTS

INTRODUCTION by the Author

As a small boy I began to enjoy reading short stories especially those with plenty of pictures. The "Topsy and Tim" series were my favourite, until one day I was given a small booklet by my parents. Full of colourful cartoon drawings, it looked very exciting with the cover showing two small buses suspended from a fairground carousel – roundabout - wonderfully illustrated with a cheerful crowd of people celebrating. The little story book was actually a timetable leaflet entitled, "Going Your Way". It was to me the best "story book" at the time, and I realised something great was coming to town. The booklet stirred my imagination, with what came across to me as the bus version of Rev. Awdrey's "Thomas the Tank Engine" stories.

Several days later, my dad took me to visit one of the buses that featured in "Going Your Way". This was my chance to see the real life character. I was full of excitement, for despite it being a dark damp dreary evening, we made our way to Crofton Road beside the railway station to find amongst the puddles a small friend waiting for people to greet "her": there sat OV3 with "Tornado" proudly inscribed on her sides. It took no time for me to realise that this was something special, appealing to all the senses. Climbing inside I was instantly greeted by a joyful new aroma: the delight of plush purple seating and soft dark grey carpeted walls. I could *taste* the newness of the bus! After this introduction, it was no wonder that I developed great enthusiasm and regard for Roundabout. This bus clearly had an impact on me, as from that day onwards, my great passion and interest for all things buses commenced: in a word Roundabout was quite simply *"friendly"*, and all I ever wanted to do was to become a Roundabout bus driver.

As the new buses became familiar sights in Orpington, the new buzz words for me were "Optare" and "Robin Hood", for these warm names focused my aspirations to comprehend people and their social interaction. From onboard a Roundabout bus, I soon became acquainted with everyday life and watched and learned with great interest the very kind etiquette between passenger and driver. A flower seller's call of "A Pound a Bunch!" evokes memories aboard a Roundabout bus as we traversed the High Street! For me, "Optare" and "Robin Hood" certainly beat "Topsy" and "Tim" hands down!

4   **Tom Gurney,**   **Petts Wood,**   **June 2010**

Above: The author aged 4, after his first ride on a Roundabout bus, RH8 'Swan', on route R3, posing at Green Street Green, on the inaugural day of the new Orpington network, 16th August 1986. *Photo: K. Gurney*

Below: Inspiring youngsters – an extract from the "Going Your Way" 1986 publicity.

Foreword by Karl Gurney

My father's 1951 diary carries an entry a few days before his only son's third birthday "Karl recognised *all* the bus route numbers at the War Memorial today!" As we walked over Chislehurst commons, a stone's throw from home, I couldn't wait to feast my eyes upon these gorgeous gleaming red giants parked up opposite the memorial. These of course carried the numbers 161, while those running across the traffic lights showed just 61. Then there were the single deckers which came up from Chislehurst High Street and peeled right - 227 - or left - 228 - at the lights. So my father's novel efforts to teach me numeracy backfired somewhat, for he unwittingly nurtured his son's latent love of all things buses! Lessons in literacy (and geography) followed, naturally by reading destination blinds, but visits to friends in Mottingham revealed that route 124, 126 & 161 intermediates all read the same – "ELTHAM MOTTINGHAM"– a post war economy trait!

By the time our sons came along, nursery schooling had become a means of teaching pre-school children numeracy and literacy. Never-the-less, the boys were introduced to public transport from a very early age; indeed our youngest was brought home to Petts Wood on a 284 bus a few days after his birth in Farnborough Hospital! As well as running in the blood, buses were now in the genes: their maternal great grandfather had been a bus driver for much of his 51 year service with LPTB and LT. Little wonder all three sons became bus enthusiasts! After leaving Coopers School, Tom attended Orpington College where he obtained GNVQ in Leisure & Tourism. His dream to become a Roundabout driver of course vanished in 1995 at age 13, but he enjoyed the opportunity to drive a front engined bus over a former Roundabout route (R2) whilst with Tellings Golden Miller, whose General Manager acknowledged Tom's achievement in "providing a friendly service" with accolades two months running as "Driver of the Month"! Whilst with Metrobus, Tom had the honour of driving the inaugural Dart on route R7.

The late 1970s and early 1980s brought great change to bus service provision in the UK, as government White Papers sought to deregulate and privatise the industry nationwide. Furthermore, New Bus Grant became available only for "off the peg" models, eliminating the capital's tried and tested practice of designing buses, such as the Routemaster, to meet its own demanding needs. It was during this time that I became involved with passenger representation, inevitably bumping into Bryan Constable, who was Engineering Manager at the newly formed Selkent District. Our first meeting was not entirely harmonious, for I was part of a delegation from the London Transport Passengers Committee, which was somewhat incensed by the increasing "no bus available" scenario caused by "off the peg" vehicles predominant in the London fleets.

Unbeknown to Bryan, his inquisitor actually was entirely sympathetic, for how does one defend the incidence of Fleetline gearbox components depositing themselves on the tarmac on the first day of service? With a great deal of courtesy, Bryan calmly outlined Selkent's plans to acquire more robust types with some urgency, such as Leyland Nationals for TB, but placed us on oath to keep secret his scheme to evaluate the new Titans and MCWs side by side at SP!

As Bryan rose to become Selkent's District General Manager, our meetings became more frequent, and I developed great respect for this dedicated and forthright gentleman. However, until my son Tom, the author, decided to document the "Roundabout" story - the operation which had made such an impression at a very early age - I had no idea just how instrumental Bryan had been in this localised small bus enterprise. It has been a delight to witness Tom and Bryan liaise over the production of this book, revealing in the process so much "behind the scenes" activity. Indeed, we are deeply indebted to Bryan for freely imparting hitherto embargoed information for inclusion, while many former employees have eagerly come forward with information, anecdotes and photographs.

Roundabout magnificently reversed the 1970s/1980s trend which regarded bus travel as "the poor man's way of getting about". One Prime Minister at the time held the view "One has failed if one still uses buses by the age of thirty". Roundabout ridiculed this by successfully appealing to socio-economic categories perhaps thought lost to buses forever. Because of the localised and frequent nature, London commuters could reliably depend on the new small buses for railheading, while many a small child, enchanted by the miniature, intimate nature of the RH and OV, succeeded in persuading mummy to go for a bus ride to the shops, leaving family auto on the driveway!

In being requested to provide historical notes and photographs from the period, it has been a privilege to plunder records and photographs from a personal lifelong collection. In particular, I was pleased Tom chose a selection of photos which also capture local people and their surroundings, thereby including a snapshot of the environment served by Roundabout. I hope they complement the enthusiasm and dedication Tom has devoted in the following pages.

KARL GURNEY
Former Member London Transport Passengers Committee
Former Vice-chair Orpington District Rail Passengers Association

Preface by Bryan Constable

Having read the proof sheets of this book, I am mindful that it sounds as though Roundabout, once the contract was awarded, was very much down to me. In truth it was my privilege to bring out the best in a small team of people who had many proven or latent skills and a hunger to use them to the full in order to build a successful new business.

Of course my family and I threw all our energy into the project; hardly surprising since Margaret – my wife known to many readers of this book – and I started our married life right at the centre of gravity of the proposed network and we really did know it 'like the back of our hands'.

Furthermore, I – and my workplace team – believed passionately that, following all the background consultations and adjustments to the original ideas, the LT service planning team had come up with the optimum way forward.

Moreover, the parcel of work was of a size that, were it to become for sale in the middle distance, then it was realistic to believe that we might, with the work people, be able to raise the money to buy it. Some years into the successful operation of Roundabout I was told by the Chairman of LBL that the Orpington operation would "never ever be sold off separately from Selkent as it looked like being a key element in Selkent's total value". He added quite aggressively, "Forget any ideas that you might have for siphoning it off for yourself or your mates!"

Anyway, back to the matter of getting the original show on the road. Not only was the size of the parcel of work appropriate to the needs of the area, its size was big enough:

1) to support either a complete business or a stand-alone subsidiary of a big group;

2) to make raising capital for it a good risk to bankers;

3) to justify the provision of proper operating and maintenance premises rather than just rolled hardcore on a bomb site;

4) to motivate bright junior managers and supervisors to move frontiers closer to private enterprise efficiency standards;

5) to make chassis manufacturers and body builders compete aggressively for supplying well designed rolling stock at keen prices;

6) to provide its managers with an outstanding opportunity to enhance their skills and prospects for subsequent promotion to the highest levels in the industry, and

7) to enhance the TBD's reputation for professionalism, both with its immediate paymasters and national tendering authorities.

All these factors ultimately gave Roundabout a magic not enjoyed by any comparable project either before or since. People who went onto greatness through a major involvement in Roundabout in their formative years included: Peter Hendy CBE (London's Commissioner for Transport), Adrian Jones (Managing Director – First London), Peter Shulver (General Manager – London Dial-a-Ride Services), Bob Muir (Operations Director – Centre-West), Harry Chambers (Sales Director – Iveco UK), Russell Richardson (Chief Executive Officer – Optare Group) and Nick Newton (Director – Office of Rail Franchising). Other people, including myself, but too numerous to mention here, did well out of the experience and went on to Director-level posts in the engineering, finance and journalism sectors.

Pride also showed through at the sharp end of the job with Roundabout winning awards at major bus promotional events and the UK Coach Rally on many occasions. Driver David Hulls became a regular national finalist in the UK Bus Driver of the Year competition held annually at Blackpool.

Just a quick word, if I may, about my retirement for which I remember one presentation particularly clearly. It was a Roundabout driver presenting me with a 1:76 model of a Leyland National with perfect Roundabout livery and artwork, and making a very short speech thanking me for the pleasure that it had been for him and his colleagues to work at Roundabout.

That's enough for now because I would like you to read on and enjoy Tom's most interesting and informative book.

BRYAN D. CONSTABLE
BSc(Eng); CEng; MIMechE, MIRTE; MSOE
Former Director, Orpington Buses Ltd and Managing Director, Selkent

BACK IN 1972: "Ice cream vans"

The start of Minibus operation in SE London

Back in 1972, the Greater London Council (GLC) urged London Transport to deliver a fresh approach to route planning. This was in response to many requests for new services, which often foundered simply because the roads that were identified for the new links could not sustain standard bus types. With GLC sponsorship, four new low cost routes were introduced, or rather "trialled" as the publicity stated. One of these served South East London: the B1, introduced on the 21st October, to penetrate new communities that were "off the beaten track" from conventional big bus operations. The B1 was worked by two 16 seater Ford Strachan minibuses (FS) from Bromley garage (TB), between Eltham and Bromley via Elmstead Lane, serving the locals with a "driver only service", Monday to Saturday shopping hours only.

Either side of this operating window, during Monday to Friday peaks, the B1 ran every 20 minutes from New Eltham station, via Elmstead Woods station, Logs Hill and Pines Road to Bickley station, appropriately timed for connecting trains where possible. An hourly evening service was also provided on Saturdays. Over sections of route that were not already served by buses, rather than install fixed bus stops, the B1 introduced a brand new term, "hail and ride", a concept informing passengers that the bus would stop by request wherever it was safe to do so.

New minibuses
for Eltham, New Eltham, Elmstead Woods and Bickley or Bromley
New route B1 starts October 21

London Transport

The timetable leaflet contained an advisory note, however, that due to sharp corners and narrowness of the road, passengers would be permitted to flag down a B1 at only a couple of nominated locations in Logs Hill. After ten months the peak hour arrangements ceased, but the shoppers' service grew to become an all day service, Eltham to Bromley. From these foundations, the B1 (later to become route 314) was the basis of a very successful experiment.

For bus drivers back in 1972, so used to the big bold image of the RT and RM, their nickname for the FS was to be "ice cream vans", and this term of endearment was not forgotten years later, though others have since described them as "bread vans" and even "milk floats". However such labelling would become key titles in the future of bus travel in the years to follow.

Meanwhile on route PB1 to the north of London, the FS type was to be replaced by slightly bigger vehicles in the shape of Rootes bodied Dodge small buses, fleet numbers A1 and A2. These two buses became instrumental in what was to be the next chapter of minibus operation in the capital, but on a far larger scale....

On 31st August 1973, almost a year into the route B1 minibus experiment, FS9 is pictured in the east side of Bromley Market Square, which was toured on all four sides en route from East Street to Widmore Road. *Photo: K. Gurney*

Before Roundabout

A Dwindling Star

The postwar expansion of bus services in the Orpington area seemed to have ground to a halt after the extension of route 94 from Petts Wood to Orpington in 1964. The difficulties experienced system-wide in London Transport buses, both Central and Country & Green Line departments, are well recorded. The 1968 reshaping plan, Busplan 78, and ultimately the Fares Fair fiduciary package of 1982, conspired to leave the outer suburbs with some very wide headway services, with certain sections of route being withdrawn evenings and or Sundays. Traffic congestion, staff shortages and "off-the-peg" buses undermined the reliability of what remained, contributing to a decline on patronage which seemingly could not be contained.

Apart from the Greater London Council (GLC) sponsored route B1, the escalating costs and operational difficulties surrounding LT therefore resulted in virtual standstill in planning matters by the late 1970s. Yet many residential areas remained considerable distance from a bus service, although LT recognised that it was desirable for residents to be within 5 minutes walk, some 400 yards, from a bus stop. Many built-up areas around Orpington were deficient in this respect, such as parts of Bickley, the Coppice Estate, Knoll, Poverest, Tubbenden, New Chelsfield, Derry Downs, Leesons Hill, and of course St Paul Cray village - abandoned since the war time diversion of route 51 via the A224.

A Plea for Poverest

A local commuter group, the Orpington District Rail Passengers Association (ODRPA), was aware that among its membership, many resident in the Poverest area were extremely desirous of a bus service to Petts Wood Station for commuting purposes, also to Orpington for shopping. The Association attempted to quantify potential ridership. In 1976, a household survey was undertaken, circulating a questionnaire targeting a sample of households in the Poverest area. By means of a further questionnaire included in a routine rail passenger survey at Petts Wood station in 1979, more information on the likely patronage of a bus service bringing Poverest area residents to Petts Wood station for rail commuting purposes was acquired.

Armed with statistics demonstrating that a 15 minute headway could be justified in the peaks, and 20 minutes during shopping periods, the Association felt confident that LT would agree the wisdom of a new / extended bus route linking Poverest with Petts Wood and Orpington. Although many representations were made, LT's response, whilst sympathetic, was invariably to conclude that financial pressures would not permit instigation of such a service, and that the onus was on consolidation in the difficult prevailing operational and financial circumstances.

Enter London Country

At a traffic forum held by a companion local Association, an LT official indicated that such a new bus service in the area might be of interest to LCBS. Images were conjured up of how twenty years earlier, LT felt that Ramsden Estate was best served by the Country Bus Department, and route 854 was born (becoming route 493)! ODRPA met officers of London Country South East, and were encouraged to learn that their Operations Manager, Andrew Braddock, had indeed identified a "deficiency corridor" in Orpington, and had in mind a service 491 from Chelsfield Station via Repton Road, Orpington High Street and Poverest Road to Petts Wood Station. There was, however, a major stumbling block because the LT fares scale would have to be adopted, and pre-paid passes and elderly persons' concessionary travel permits accepted. As was normal for LCBS services operating in the GLC area, financial support would be applied for, £13,000 in the case of a six month trial of hourly route 491 starting in September 1980. Not unexpectedly, LT was unable to authorise such a sum in those belt-tightening times.

A Pleasant Surprise

With nothing but retrenchment to look forward to after the political and judicial events in 1981/2 in the aftermath of GLC's "Fares Fair" collapse, it seemed all hope of better bus penetration anywhere was best consigned to the waste bin. However, late in 1983, a very sympathetic contact in Selkent tipped the nod that all was not lost, and to stay optimistic. True enough, for early in the new year, it was officially notified that new route 276 would be introduced the following May between Petts Wood station and Orpington station via Poverest Road, Cray Avenue and Orpington High Street, experimentally for six months. However, the new route was to run only hourly Mondays to Fridays, between 0700 and 1900. Although some account was to be taken meeting trains at Petts Wood, it raised concerns that it would be of limited use to commuters, while only those able to convene their activities around a 60 minute headway would find it viable, i.e. the bulk of passengers would be elderly persons' permit holders.

Interestingly, the Managing Director of London Buses at the time had stated at a meeting with London Regional Passengers Committee (LRPC), that he felt that daytime services at hourly headways in built-up areas were distinctly unattractive; they needed "looking at" to see if they should be running at all, and if so, then the minimum frequency passengers could expect should be half-hourly. A realisation was dawning that the public, in the closing decades of the twentieth century, was not prepared to organise itself around bus services which had become unacceptably infrequent and unreliable. Route 61, for example, had become non-clockface at 24/25 minute headway during shopping hours. Furthermore, many routes serving Orpington were second or third journey projections at 20 or 30 minute intervals, having encountered traffic congestion through notorious centres (notably Bromley) en route from terminals such as Lewisham and Woolwich. Staff and vehicle shortages also took their toll, and there seemed little incentive to ensure the dependability of timetables. If the last bus was cut or ran ten minutes early, nobody seemed to care. Never-the-less, route 276 was a start, and for the first time in twenty years, an additional line was to be drawn on the bus map of Orpington.

The route began on 14th May 1984, and was actually numbered 284 to reflect its year of birth, requiring a single LS vehicle from Bromley Garage. In fact two vehicles would appear on the route each day, as drivers took their breaks at TB, running in service beyond Orpington station via route 61. The two buses would pass each other in Locks Bottom, and occasionally, the second vehicle would be a double deck Titan, complete with blinds for route 284. This short route quickly established a reputation for reliability, but as feared, it took a brave commuter to rely on an hourly bus to go to the station to catch a train to London in the morning. However, the 1808 ex-Petts Wood was usually very well patronised by homegoing commuters. Predictably, the 284 was immensely popular amongst the elderly, and the 0900-ex Petts Wood was often full up and standing by Orpington High Street.

After one month, Selkent advised that the on-board revenue, "as distinct from passes and permits" had only reached half the required target, with little prospect of it improving. There was also concern over abstraction from neighbouring routes. Headcounts would be conducted towards the end of the trial. Never-the-less, the six month trial period came and went, and the 284 soldiered on. Just before Christmas, local posters advised that on days over the holiday period when Saturday services would prevail (December 24 / 27 / 28 / 31), happily route 284 would run to its normal Monday – Friday timetable.

The 1984 Orpington Review: Innovative Proposals

The "experimental" Poverest Road service continued into 1985. Soon after surviving its first birthday, route 284 became officially considered successful, along with route 493 (Orpington – Ramsden Estate circular), owing to the localised nature of these routes. Such were the findings of a review revealed in the Spring in a revolutionary package by LRT entitled "Proposals for the Orpington Bus Network".

LRT had seen how reducing the cost of individual bus routes had been achieved by offering them out to competitive tender. For example, during 1985, route 146 (Bromley North – Downe) was awarded to Crystals from 20th August, being among the first batch of routes subject to this process. Motivated by the need to contain costs, yet improve the quantity, coverage and reliability of bus services, LRT went on to draw up the first major tranche of routes in a *whole area* to be operated on a tendered basis. Orpington was chosen for this "pilot" scheme for two reasons.

Firstly, it appears that route 284 was not the only local route to undergo headcounts in 1984, for the availability of such up-to-date data collected that same year for *all* Bromley area routes was a contributing factor in opting for Orpington.

Secondly Orpington was served by a number of operators, viz London Buses, London Country South East, and independents such as Metrobus and Crystals. LRT felt it should exercise its statutory remit to ensure a network of integrated services. It effectively decided to wipe clean the bus map of Orpington, and start the planning process all over again as if bus no routes existed in the entire area.

T1113 on route 284 arrives in Petts Wood on 31st December 1985. The proud King Edward Cigar adverts, a regular feature on bus fronts of the time, have long gone, as has the K6 phone box too! *Photo: K. Gurney*

Local routes 284 and 493 were considered successful in LRT's 1984 Orpington Area Review. On a snowy 6th February 1986, LCBS green SNB 159 meets LBL red LS 412 at Orpington station. The turning circle, complete with railway semaphore signal, is now the site of the "Orpington Bus Interchange". *Photo: K. Gurney*

The proposals were sent to local authorities, passenger representatives, and other interested parties, who were invited to comment by early September 1985, following which the statutory consultation process would commence. At the time, Orpington's bus network comprised the following:

51 Woolwich – Orpington Station daily

61 Bromley North – Eltham Station daily

161 Woolwich – Sidcup Garage daily or Petts Wood Station Mon-Sat except evenings

208 Lewisham – Petts Wood daily, extended to Orpington Mon-Sat, extended Saturday shopping hours Lewisham – Surrey Docks

229 Green Street Green – Sidcup Station daily, extended to Bexleyheath except evenings and Sunday, further extended to Erith Mon-Fri peaks

261 Lewisham – Orpington daily, extended Saturday shopping hours Lewisham – Surrey Docks

284 Petts Wood Station–Orpington Station Mon-Fri except evenings

357 Orpington – East Croydon Mon-Sat except evenings

431 Orpington – Sevenoaks Mon-Sat

471 Orpington – Knockholt – Orpington Mon-Sat circular in both directions, with some journeys Orpington – Dunton Green Garage

477 Chelsfield "Five Bells" – Dartford daily

493 Orpington Station – Ramsden – Orpington Station Mon-Sat circular in both directions, with hourly journeys to Green Street Green. One journey per hour diverted to Goodmead Road instead of Station

706 Green Line Victoria - Bromley – Tunbridge Wells daily

858 Orpington – Biggin Hill Mon-Fri except evenings

The Basic Principles

The report considered that rationalisation was necessary of the three routes operating between Orpington and Bromley. Of the 28,000 journeys undertaken daily in the Orpington area, 10% were to/from Bromley. It was proposed that route 261 should be withdrawn between Bromley and Orpington, leaving routes 61 and 208 as the trunk services between the two centres. Furthermore, because just 5% of journeys were made to/from Eltham, and to improve its reliability, route 61 would be split into two sections, viz. high frequency (10-15 minute headway) 61A Bromley – Orpington, and 61B Orpington – Eltham. It was also revealed that 8% of journeys were undertaken to/from Sidcup, with 5% travelling to/from Bexleyheath / Woolwich. It was therefore considered that route 229 should be withdrawn between Green Street Green and Sidcup. Truncation of routes 229 and 261 would release resources to help fund the proposed network of local services modelled on routes 284 and 493. The new network would introduce smaller buses for economic reasons and to access areas not currently served by buses on practical grounds. The study considered that small buses would be more acceptable than traditional double deckers to residents in areas hitherto unserved, and would enable higher frequencies to be offered on routes currently operated by conventional buses. Most importantly, the localised network would be reliable in being segregated from the major traffic congestion elsewhere in the suburbs.

A Network of Local Routes

Using the prefix "L" for convenience at this stage, five local routes were proposed. Route L1 featuring small buses at 5-6 minute headway during the day (20 minutes evenings and Sundays) Green Street Green – St Pauls Cray estate would replace double deck routes 261 and 229, which were running at 20 minute intervals during the day, half-hourly at other times. Passengers affected by the loss of a through route to Bromley would be expected to change into routes 61A / 208 in Orpington High Street. Route L1 would terminate as close as possible to the route 51 Midfield Way stop in Sevenoaks Way in order to effect interchange for estate passengers travelling to Foots Cray and beyond. Route 51 would remain a trunk route Orpington Station – Woolwich, likewise route 208 Orpington – Lewisham. Routes 357 Orpington – Croydon and 858 Orpington – Biggin Hill would remain unaltered, and route 477 from Dartford would acquire a slight change in the Chelsfield area. Routes 208 and 477 would be excluded from the invitations to tender.

18

Route L2 was intended to replace route 493 between Ramsden Estate and Orpington, but would continue to use large single deckers (Leyland Nationals) at 15 minute intervals during the day. Buses would continue alternately to Orpington Station, or via Orpington High Street, St Mary Cray High Street and Main Road to Chalk Pit Avenue in St Pauls Cray. Route L2 would restore a bus service in St Pauls Cray village, lost since 1939 when industries located along the A224 Sevenoaks Way contributing to the war effort caused route 51 to be (permanently) rerouted away from the Cray villages. During peak periods, the St Pauls Cray journeys would double-run via Orpington Station. Only an hourly service was proposed in the evenings and Sundays, all journeys double running via Orpington Station.

Proposed route L3 bore a strong resemblance to LCBS's route 491 aspirations five years earlier. Route L3 would run from Petts Wood station via route 284 to the end of Poverest Road, thence via Kent Road, Lower Road, Orpington High Street, Sevenoaks Road, Repton Road, Eton Road and The Highway to Chelsfield Station. A 20 minute interval was envisaged during the day, representing a considerable frequency increase over route 284, achieved by deploying small buses, which would penetrate the New Chelsfield area for the first time. A Saturday service would feature, plus a trial hourly weekday evening service. In consequence, route 284 would be withdrawn. The arrangements were considered adequate replacement for route 493 in the Chelsfield station area.

To compensate for the loss of a link between Farnborough and Orpington caused by withdrawal of route 261 south of Bromley, route L4 was proposed to run from Pallant Way, Locks Bottom, via route 261 to Farnborough village, then Farnborough Way and Tubbenden Lane. During Monday to Friday peaks, route L4 would terminate at Orpington Station on a 12 minute headway. At other times it would continue via Orpington High Street to terminate at the Goodmead Road 261 stand, every 15 minutes during shopping hours, hourly in the evenings, and half-hourly on Sundays.

Proposed routes L5 and L6 were intended to halt the decline in the country routes serving the villages to the south of Orpington. By 1985, route 471 was offering a few with-flow peak period journeys between Dunton Green and Orpington, and just three "traditional" circular journeys in each direction during Monday to Friday shopping periods. On Saturdays, a few circular journeys plied in each direction during the day, with a late night bus from Orpington to Dunton Green garage via Cudham and Knockholt. A service approximately every two hours ran on route 431 between Orpington and Sevenoaks via Chelsfield Village, Badgers Mount, Halstead, Knockholt and Dunton Green.

The proposals envisaged withdrawal of routes 431 and 471 to be replaced by Monday to Saturday routes L5 and L6. A single small bus was proposed to operate hourly circuits from Green Street Green via Cudham, Knockholt Pound and Rushmore Hill to Green Street Green as route L5, then outbound again, but as route L6, from Green Street Green via Badgers Mount, Halstead, Knockholt Pound and Rushmore Hill to Green Street Green. Passengers for Orpington would need to change at Green Street Greet into route L1, except during peak periods, when through services would run to/from Orpington Station, with "big" buses appearing on some route L6 journeys. In the morning peak, route L5 would operate in the reverse direction, but for the rest of the day, the common L5/L6 section Knockholt Pound – Green Street Green via Rushmore Hill would receive two journeys per hour. No service was proposed in the evenings or on Sundays. The proposals specifically mentioned "Waitrose" as the shopping objective for these villages, with "the green opposite Glentrammon Road" as the terminus.

Route 477 would be extended from the "Five Bells" at Chelsfield, to operate loop fashion via Maypole to replace route 431 in Greater London, while the Kent section of route 431 between Halstead, Knockholt Pound and Sevenoaks would be replaced by diverting route 706.

Consultation

The proposals were offered to interested parties, who were invited to comment by 6th September 1985. However, the proposals mentioned a number of variations to the local routes, and views on the desirability of these were also welcomed. These included a peak hour diversion to route L1 via Station Road / Tower Road to bring the route nearer Orpington Station, and running all journeys on routes L5 and L6 to Orpington town centre at the "new" stand in Gravel Pit Way but at two hourly intervals, with an option to revise the direction of loop operation. Route L3 could be extended beyond Chelsfield Station to serve Windsor Drive, terminating in the vicinity of Foxbury Drive, High Beeches and Daleside. An alternative to routeing via Repton Road would be to use Charterhouse Road instead. A favoured option for route L4 would be to use Starts Hill Road between Locks Bottom and Farnborough, thus providing same stop interchange between route L4 and 61A to/from Bromley.

Consultation largely engendered support for the proposed improved coverage, although predictably, some prejudice was levelled against buses. The use of Tubbenden Lane by buses was derided by some, who apparently recalled a previous occasion when buses used this road with an inspector positioned at the railway bridge to stop traffic on the approach of a bus! There was some hostility in Repton Road and the streets envisaged for turning buses should route L3 use Windsor Drive. Representations were made to keep a service hitherto provided by route 493 via Warren Road, Chelsfield Station and Green Street Green. Strong protests were made regarding the need to make a hazardous change between routes 51 and L1 at Midfield Way / Sevenoaks Way. Farnborough residents were enraged at the prospect of their link with Bromley being reduced to an hourly service on Green Line 706. Splitting route 61 in Orpington attracted various critics. The North Downs villagers indicated a clear preference for their link with Orpington to be maintained throughout the day. After due consideration, LRT amended their proposals and the final network, in which the local routes changed their prefix to "R", firmed up towards the end of 1985. Invitations to tender were then published, the results of which being announced in April 1986 for introduction in August.

The Network Firms Up

Route R1 was to operate at 15 minute intervals Green Street Green – Queen Marys Hospital, thus avoiding the need for St Pauls Cray estate passengers to change at Midfield Way / Sevenoaks Way en route to/from Sidcup. A second section of route R1 was added also at 15 minute headway to operate from Grovelands in St Pauls Cray estate to Green Street Green, then via Farnborough village and Locks Bottom to Bromley Common. The Crown Lane Spur stand at Bromley Common would be shared with routes 208 and 261, thus offering greater scope for connections to/from Bromley. The two sections were timetabled to interwork at 7/8 minute headway over the common sector. During evenings and Sundays, route R1 would run Bromley Common – Queen Marys Hospital throughout at 20 minute intervals. A further concession was offered Farnborough residents in the form an additional "big" bus route 261A, becoming Metrobus 361 upon introduction, running hourly Monday to Saturday, evenings excepted, Green Street Green – Bromley North.

The L2 proposal was dropped entirely, but the route number R2 was assigned to route 858. Ramsden estate would continue to be operated by modified route 493.

Route R3 was specified, as proposed, at 20 minute intervals, with an extension (evenings excepted) via the whole length of Windsor Drive to Green Street Green, with one further extension to the 2240 ex-Petts Wood Saturday night to Cudham and Knockholt Pound to replace the isolated late night journey on route 471. In the morning peak, route R3 would double run via Orpington Station northbound, and southbound during the evening peak. The hourly evening service, introduced experimentally, would operate via the station in both directions.

Starts Hill Road was adopted for route R4 on departing from Pallant Way, but owing to the presence of routes R1 and 361 serving Farnborough, route R4 would run via Farnborough Way to Tubbenden Lane. It would then operate via Orpington Station northbound (southbound journeys omitted the station), Orpington High Street then via proposed route L2 to Pauls Cray Hill. A half-hourly Monday to Saturday service was introduced, with no service after 1830.

Route R5 acknowledged the wish for the villagers to remain linked with Orpington, and basically perpetuated the same routeing as the 471, with journeys operating from Orpington Station at improved (hourly) intervals running alternately clockwise / anticlockwise around the Cudham – Knockholt Pound – Rushmore Hill loop. Additional peak / school journeys would be operated by a "Big" single deck bus (an LS vehicle from Bromley Garage).

Perhaps surprisingly, route 431 was to be replicated by Monday to Saturday route R6, which would run, albeit infrequently, from Orpington Station via Warren Road, Chelsfield Station, Chelsfield village, Badgers Mount, Halstead, Knockholt Pound and Dunton Green to Sevenoaks. Just a few Green Line 706 journeys would be diverted via Halstead and Knockholt Pound en route to/from Sevenoaks, while a number of peak journeys on route R5 would also operate via Halstead.

Tender results for the "big" buses revealed that Metrobus had retained route 357, and won route 61, which was the route number to be retained for the Bromley – Chislehurst section of the original through route, at 12-15 minute headway, thus eliminating the division at Orpington; however route 61 continued to work through to Eltham on Sundays. The residual Monday to Saturday Chislehurst – Eltham section became double decked half-hourly route 61B and was won by Selkent. Route 51 was awarded to London Country which also retained the remains of route 493, Orpington Station – Ramsden estate circular.

Ken Glazier: a True Gentleman

The network of small bus operated local routes was awarded as an entity to "Roundabout", a closely guarded enterprise created by LBL's Selkent District. Before revealing more about this hard earned success, it is poignant at this stage to pause to pay tribute to a true gentleman whom Selkent was privileged to have as an outstanding consultant on its traffic and service planning side. He was the respected transport historian and book-editor extraordinaire, Ken Glazier. Consistent with his track record of treating all pressure groups with genuine courtesy (not least because he passionately believed in never letting any incoming information go to waste), as soon as the tendering results were announced he insisted on a meeting with ODRPA to review the network plans from a customer perspective. How has LRT's revamp been received by its users? Have the replacements covered the area sufficiently, providing links and at times people actually required? How did the maths add up replacing 70 seat double deckers at 20 minute headway (210 seats per hour) with 21 seat midibuses at 7-8 minute headway (168 seats per hour) through St Pauls Cray estate?

Already thinking to the future, plans for even greater coverage, capacity and frequency "going your way" were being considered, as manifest throughout the following years, with Ken, Bryan Constable and their team at the Roundabout helm until privatisation.

After leaving the bus industry, Ken Glazier produced a wealth of publications based on his extensive knowledge. Sadly, this flow ceased after 2007 when this true gentleman passed away after so short a time in "retirement".

St Pauls Cray estate was generating more than enough passengers to justify the capacity provided by route double deck route 229, as evidenced by M802 in Cray Avenue, 26th October 1984. How would the replacement midibuses cope with a 20% reduction in seats on offer? *Photo: K. Gurney*

Right: a pre-production Roundabout bus stop "E"-plate sticker, devised when the network was shaping up in the planning office.

Below: the Orpington area route map from 16th August 1986 as illustrated in the "Going Your Way" booklet.

Behind the Scenes

The Tender Bid

In 1985, London Regional Transport felt that Orpington would become "a major focus of attention in the bus industry", for the Orpington network was to be the first instance of a whole area's routes being put out to competitive tender.

Clearly with several operators in the Orpington area (Selkent, London Country Bus Services, Crystals and Metrobus), not to mention the possibility of any new operators coming along to apply to the Tendered Bus Division (TBD) for inclusion on the list to tender for the Orpington bus network, it was not surprising that London Buses (LBL) and their associated operating districts (in this instance Selkent) were eager not to lose out to independent operators. It was calculated that 172 jobs at LBL were at risk; therefore it was paramount to take a fresh look at demonstrating modern bus operating practice. The whole package involved work for 80 buses, 55 of which were currently LBL operated. The small bus proposals were worth 24 vehicles alone.

Metrobus had been keen for many years to operate a bus route along Tubbenden Lane and would no doubt tender for the L4 and possibly the whole group of routes. Indeed, divulged years later was Metrobus' idea of using short bodied Bedford single deckers, deciding not to conform to the midibus revolution. The fact that the "R"-prefix routes eventually graduated to Dennis Darts would suggest that Metrobus' judgement was correct, if not a few years too early.

Not surprisingly, 55 Broadway had a special project ready and waiting, which was put to the drawing board with the aim of winning the "package of goods", with special focus on the small bus network.

Bryan Constable was District General Manager at Selkent District based at One, Warner Road, Camberwell. He had been on a one year secondment as General Manager at Aldenham works. Despite having so much weight on his shoulders, he was seen as the ideal man for a new project, and was approached by chiefs at 55 Broadway. Bryan was asked to work up a "play to win strategy" that was to be "an innovative commercially aggressive bid for the TBD's Orpington small bus network". He therefore set about organising such a compliant bid, with a clear aim to see if a new company could be formed out of it.

Relieved of his Aldenham responsibilities, Bryan was given the time and freedom to work on this important project and was invited to nominate two assistants to help with the groundwork. Bob Muir, on a fast track management course, and Peter Hendy, a former graduate trainee in his first "real" job in personnel management, were to plan pay and conditions, together with organising the recruitment process and uniform designs. Bob and Peter were also delegated the task of seeking out potential operating bases and completing all the planning consent paperwork.

Bryan proceeded with costing a tender application for the six small bus routes (L1, L3, L4, L5, L6 and 858). The tender proposals were put forward in the name of Orpington Buses Limited t/a "Rising Star Buses", with a fleet of twenty-five Mercedes 609s in a proposed livery of chocolate and custard, famously associated with the highly respected former Great Western Railway. Certainly, the fashionable 1980s trend for inclusion of devices such as "go faster stripes" in livery design was felt should be consigned to the "Yuppie" areas of Chelsea and Docklands, and would not be appreciated by the socio-economic categories which "Rising Star" would be serving in Orpington!

The Mercedes 608D operating Crystals route 858. This vehicle type would have been commonplace on Rising Star Buses.

Photo: E.L. Collinson

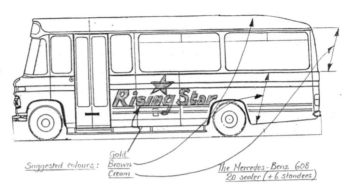

An early sketch by Bryan Constable, showing how the "Rising Star" livery might be applied to the Reeves Burgess Mercedes midibus.

Suggested colours: Gold Brown Cream

The Mercedes-Benz 608 20 seater (+ 6 standees)

As former Head of Distribution Services with responsibility for the London Transport goods vehicle fleet, Bryan's knowledge of fleet management and in-depth vehicle specifications meant he was able realistically to cost the use of "van like" commercial vehicles. He had access to detailed costs of large "panel vans" (vehicles that were many in number used for auxiliary purposes within LT, such as uniform stores and parts transfers). He translated their fuel consumption and running cost data into the "stop-start" practice of daily bus operations. It was anticipated that annual mileage for the fleet would be in excess of one million miles on the six routes. A setting-up cost was identified to reflect an intention to use twenty-five Reeves Burgess bodied Mercedes vehicles.

Importantly, there was the need to assess competitors' other costs accurately in order to build up an exact figure that Rising Star ideally had to beat or equal. Selkent's premises guru, by scaling competitors' premises sizes (including proportions of covered and open parking) to its own garages, calculated the commercial rates that Rising Star had to come in under. A corresponding exercise on wages and operating efficiency in units of *seat-miles per pound of staff costs* was judicially applied to Metrobus and London Country South-East.

It can now be revealed that Rising Star set itself the task of producing at least 34% more mileage per £ of gross costs than that of its red bus partners. Its cost model achieved this by such a huge margin that the Selkent management had some jitters about the accuracy of the arithmetic. However, the synthetic costs that went into the bid held up throughout the life of the contracts. Roundabout, as it became known, made genuine profits – not massive but around the private enterprise norm. This vindicated all the financial homework.

The Announcement

Bryan's bid was successful, and LRT awarded a three year contract for all six local routes, announced on the 10th April 1986. Bryan lost no time in setting up the new firm, Orpington Buses Ltd., with the assistance of LT's lawyers. It was to be an independent company wholly owned by LT under the banner of Selkent District.

At a time when bus employees were somewhat puzzled by the tendering regime, and subdued by the resulting fragmentation of "their" network, Bryan helped define the way forward to keep work "in house" by creating subsidiary undertakings in different guises such as Orpington Buses Ltd. Speaking to "LT News" staff magazine, Bryan went on to explain, "We beat some very strong competition for these routes and our success is a major breakthrough .... and if we do not get in on the act now a further significant part of the company's operations could be put at risk".

A Done Deal

The original Rising Star Buses tender application was costed with the idea of Mercedes 608D minibuses, similar to the type used by Crystals on the 858. This should have been the cheapest of three options, the other two being with twenty-five Dodge or twenty-five Optare. However, just at Roundabout's vehicle procurement stage, Mercedes announced that its model 608D would be withdrawn from the market pending a major upgrade. A gap now appeared in the cost comparisons:

MODEL	PURCHASE PRICE	LEASE PRICE per annum
MERCEDES 608D / REEVE BURGESS 20 seat	Withdrawn from market	£5,676
DODGE 50 S56C / ROOTES 19 seat	£23,000	£7,105
OPTARE VW CITY PACER LT55 25 seat	£25,400	£7,786

Happily, however, news had spread on the trade grape vine that a new midibus operation was to begin with LT. Bryan was approached by a very keen Iveco salesman, Harry Chambers (ultimately to become Iveco's UK Sales Director), who was desperate to get his company into the capital's bus scene. With an offer too good to turn down, Bryan accepted Iveco's excellent deal based on their 49/10 underfame, which meant the Roundabout fleet was going to cost a lot less than they had planned for, hence the operation was "quids in" before they had even started!

Bryan went out of his way to achieve an aim: to eradicate fears of cheap tacky vehicles often seen as "breadvans". But by 1986, a new word was on the bus market: no more minibuses, but purpose built "midibuses" were the way forward. Optare was a leader in purpose built construction, with their Optare City Pacer LT55 (OV), and MCW following a year later with their Metrorider design. Ultimately the public's view of cheap looking minibus vehicles was hopefully to be laid to rest with the introduction of these new stylish models.

Vehicle Risks.... Buying in a Hurry

Despite this rapidly unfolding trend, Iveco did not have a purpose built small bus on the drawing board, but their 49/10 chassis - interestingly rather tougher than the Mercedes equivalent - was earmarked by west country operators as having the potential to take a coach built midibus body with a capacity of about 20 seats. Iveco informed Bryan and his Engineering Director designate that a Solent factory associated with motorboats had built a very small number of trial midibuses on the 49/10 underframe, and recommended that the "Roundabout" team take a serious look at the results. Suitably impressed, Bryan ordered 24 of the vehicles that he and his colleague had inspected. Robbie Hood, who owned the factory, was looking for production volumes for something his skilled staff could build, at the same time as creating profits that could underpin international speed boat racing as a related leisure business. The bodywork name for these new buses was affectionately known by the nickname "Robin Hood"!

Bryan clearly recalls being criticised by LT's top level contracts professionals for his alleged "sloppy order"! To cut a long story short, Bryan considered he triumphed over bureaucracy "breaking one more mould at a stroke" by replacing the standard LT 30 page purchase contract by one economical A4 sized letter!

Meanwhile Optare of Leeds was producing its purpose built midi bus, the concept being the brainchild of dynamic boss Russell Richardson, who had earlier rescued the old Charles Roe coachbuilders' factory from closure. Optare's City Pacer's appearance was striking and LT's hierarchy loved it: the model LT55 was a user's midibus and its good looks made it a proven passenger traffic generator. Anyway Roundabout had promised to take delivery of five at a premium price and the TBD paid the difference in both capital and running costs.

Setting up

Given a remarkably free hand, Bryan effectively created the new company as he wanted it, and set about presenting the buses as small characters in their own right. To make things more identifiable for passengers and drivers alike, each bus carried a "pet name". Bryan believed that if buses carried individual names, they would be seen as something to admire by younger people, as opposed to vandalising them. Spray can paint and felt tip markers were becoming popular tools of graffiti "artists" and it was reportedly costing LT a lot of money in removal and anti-vandalism measures for big bus operations. Amongst the Constable family some thought was put into naming. Bryan's 14 year old son, Matthew, was given the honour of deciding the themes. Matthew settled on 24 bird species for the RH type, however, as composition of the small bus fleet was to include some Optare City Pacers, he decided upon the names of five windstorms for the OVs. The fortunes of the four RHs diverted from the Roundabout order are recorded in "History of the Robin Hoods" (page 102). "Family" was the ethos of this new company; it was to be a family run firm in terms of a welcoming, friendly local service, intending to create a great rapport between staff and passengers.

The Magic Roundabout

Dereck Keeler, LT Development Director, was keen to seek advice from a marketing agency for some ideas of how best to brand and show off the new company. There was more than a little concern that Bryan's idea of "Rising Star Buses" would be highly embarrassing if the proposed company ran into difficulties soon after its launch. The agency agreed and came back with a few ideas. The cult children's TV show, "The Magic Roundabout", was something that was felt to fit the bill well, as the new company was all about being family friendly and cuddly in context, with the buses being like toys.

The general message that was to be carried across was that the new network of routes would be going round and round the conurbation, picking up and dropping off people. This was happily agreed by LT (with perhaps the odd exception). So, "Roundabout" it was to be!

The trading name, changed to Roundabout, tied-in well with a publicity campaign that was to be launched in the form of "Roundabout Going Your Way". The agency also strongly recommended the maroon and grey livery, similar to Her Majesty's the Queen Mother Daimler DS420 company car, believing these were modern colours of the era, compatible with aspiring to the "GWR brown and cream quality ethos". They say pictures speak louder than words, and the front cover of the initial timetable booklet projected the company's desired friendly and family image. Indeed the "LT News" staff magazine reporting the tender results described the news as "swings and roundabouts for Orpington!" Often debated by staff and passengers alike, did the "R"-route numbering prefix stand for **R** OUNDABOUT, or did it stand for O **R** PINGTON ?

A suitable Operating Centre

As a former St Mary Cray resident, Bryan was keen to utilise his local knowledge to establish the new bus company in a dominant local position, and after consultation with the local council regarding several options for a base, it was deemed that an available warehouse on a brownfield site at Nugent Industrial Estate, off Cray Avenue on the outskirts of Orpington, would be most likely to receive the planning permission required, and quickly at that. It was as an ideal cost effective way to serve as an operating centre for Roundabout. As a "spin-off", the trade neighbours such as Payless, Plumb Centre, McDougall Rose (paints), Cimex (industrial cleaners) and Tilemates were delighted with the prospect that Roundabout's 24/7 operations would give them added "security" presence.

The washing of vehicles and repairs were to be kept in-house at the new base, utilising a good sturdy brush and a portable jet wash(!), with fuelling done at the nearby Petrol station at Ruxley Corner with the use of fuel cards for clear identification of each bus. If that petrol station had run out of supplies, buses would be sent at night time to the filling station along Perry Street, near Chislehurst.

Operator's Licence

Whilst the vehicle procurement, garaging and staffing issues were being pursued, so too was the matter of obtaining an Operator's Licence. Bryan and Peter put together the application and expected a quick "rubber stamp" decision; after all, Selkent's disciplinary record was clean and several of the implementation team had full Certificate of Professional Competence (CPC).

However, as recalled by Bryan, "a smooth passage it was not to be". Bryan was informed via an unorthodox route that the Metropolitan Traffic Commissioner wanted to see him. "Odd that the message should come this way", thought the Roundabout team. When Bryan presented himself at the Bromyard Avenue offices, he was asked what *he* wanted to talk to the Commissioner about! A meeting did take place, revealing that the Commissioner was clearly displeased, if not enraged, that he had not been made aware of Roundabout's ambitious plan at an earlier stage, either by London Buses or its Selkent District. In particular he criticised the fact that the trade press had published the name of the proposed Roundabout General Manager, ex-Continental Pioneer Tim Lewis, before he had cleared the selection.

In short, the Commissioner indicated that he would grant a licence if the local manager was a LT "home-grown" individual and not an external appointment. He added that Roundabout already appeared to be taking risks, and he was adamant that he would not be party to a "bridge too far" that could fail.

Peter Hendy reasoned with Bryan that since they had got their own way with just about everything else, this was not a matter worth "going to the barricades" over. Consequently, Peter Shulver was moved from Sidcup garage, where he was already doing a very good job, and posted to Roundabout, displacing Tim Lewis. One could say that the subsequent performance of Roundabout might have made the Commissioner feel good about his involvement in a LT domestic matter.

New Image

Condensed into a few words, Bryan's brief from his bosses was to achieve a completely new image from this tendering win. The new organisation was to be "something so unlike a traditional London bus company". As the first new Roundabout bus was built and ready for early collection well ahead of the tender start date, Bryan was eager to show it off to his bosses at 55 Broadway.

Robin Hood Iveco – ready for the small bus network

Pictured outside 55 Broadway is the Robin Hood Iveco which is to go into service on most of the small bus network in Orpington. The name on the side – 'Roundabout' – is the new off-shoot of London Buses formed to run the operation. Another midibus – the Optare – is being considered for two of the routes on the new network.

Asked how things were going, Bryans 'nostalgic head' had clearly placed its mark on the new bus, RH1 "Kestrel", for it was complete with "OB 1" metal garage code and running number stencils in traditional LT bracket holders, just visible in the "LT News" press cutting opposite.

The reaction from his seniors was said to be a firm "No!" to such "ephemera", disliked by them, for the simple reason that it was seen as too in keeping with outdated LT practices!

As a result, RH1 was unique in being the only Roundabout bus from new to have a double piece stencil holder fitted either side. No further stencils or bracket holders were produced and all subsequent OV/RH deliveries did not carry holders. However, some headway was made to at least accept the display of running numbers by way of identification, and thus modern black on yellow running number plates were positioned rather untidily into sides of dashboards. Eventually by early 1987, single piece running number brackets were positioned either side of the vehicles.

Operating Staff Recruitment

With the vehicle orders in place and production started, the next thing was recruitment of staff, with the main emphasis on attracting new people to the industry. Local employment officers were guided to look for people with retail experience who wanted to earn more money and were already used to dealing with the public and speedy cash handling. Fifty drivers were required, and prospective candidates new to the industry were paid a mere £16 per day whilst training for their PSV class 3 licence. Once qualified, they would be taking home average earnings of £133 over a 5 day week of 42 and-a-half hours. No shifts exceeded 9 hours driving (quite innovative in 1986), and the earliest sign-on was to be 0510 with the last duty signing-off at 0040. Duties were allocated by rota on a Monday to Saturday basis, leaving Sundays as an optional overtime facility for drivers. Sunday shifts were six and-a-half hours in duration and paid at £30 per duty.

The Trade Unions were never informed of the Rising Star blueprint on the basis that:

> it was not expected that in the available time-frame, they would agree to the necessary increase in productivity;

- the size of the operation was, on its own, unlikely to destabilize the well consolidated conditions of the 20,000 or so London red bus staff;

- if the plans were to be completely derailed by Trade Union action, then LT could protect its customers by simply surrendering all the work to competitors.

Eventually, Bryan recalls the stance of the trade union was, to quote their exact words at the time, "We note what you're doing, and why, but if you don't succeed, you cannot expect us to pull your chestnuts out of the fire".

Initially, training was conducted in-house with an Iveco (RH), with tests taking place at the official Department of Transport Test Centre in Croydon. However, there was a rather devastating spate of failures, and in response to the poor pass rates, the Selkent training school at Catford garage took over the responsibilities of training and testing new candidates.

Although there was some public concern that Roundabout would consist of young drivers on cheap wages and with little or no experience of driving, let alone bus driving, such fears were unfounded. In fact, Roundabout provided a gentle transition from crew to OPO for those that were interested. Many early one-person-operated (OPO) red bus drivers found the move from driving a crew bus to a physically bigger bus, *and* simultaneously having to make up to 400 cash transactions in one shift, just too much to cope with (at that time, there was nothing like the level of prepayment that there is today). Thus, several older gentlemen were recruited, experienced PSV holders from Sidcup Garage (SP) and Peckham (PM), looking to enjoy a more relaxed view to the job as distinct from the stresses of big bus work elsewhere within LT. One such character was Bert Cramer, a delightful man who retired when SP closed, but decided not to stay retired for very long. He was welcomed back by his former governor, Peter Shulver, who asked Bert "When would you like to start?" the moment his old colleague stepped through the doors of OB! SP conductors, displaced as a result of OPO conversion of route 21 in February 1986, might be interested in retraining to drive small buses. Together with a mix of female staff, the young and not so young, the drivers clearly became well acquainted with passengers. As a result many drivers happily became both route and duty bound. The friendly caring service that was advertised in the "Going Your Way" booklet really did come into fruition, by way of real life local characters: celebrities in their own right! This is what made the operation so appealing to the author as a young boy.

Engineering

Creator of the appropriate engineering support was Selkent's then District Engineering Manager, Steve Kerman. On leaving school he had joined one of LT's junior entrant training schemes and quickly progressed through the engineering ranks. This gave him a very accurate feel for the maintenance resources needed at Roundabout. Excluding cleaners/fuellers, his assessment of the engineering personnel needs was one competent fitter from the commercial motor trade, with assistance building up as the vehicles started to need more and more consumable parts. Warranty work would be undertaken by K T Trucks (Iveco) at Dartford and M V Trucks (Volkswagen) at Croydon. Throw in a five ton vehicle hoist (Omer ramp) and a decent tool kit and one had a set-up that worked like clockwork (or as they would say "worked like a roundabout"!).

After passing through inspection at Aldenham, twenty RH and five OV were duly delivered to Unit 17, "the home of Roundabout" (code name OB). The Two red Dodge (A1/A2) stayed at arms length at Catford garage to continue assisting the training programme, and served as spare operational vehicles for the Orpington network if needed.

The network was now ready for the start date and with Unit 17 being fitted-out as an operating centre, the eager little Ivecos and Optares filtered their way out of Aldenham to their new home in St Mary Cray.

Above left: RH21 "Gannet", despite being a high fleet number, was one of the earliest to come off the production line, seen awaiting application of decals, sitting happily in the sunshine at a very new Roundabout garage, unit17, Nugent estate. *Photo: E.L. Collinson.*
Above right: RH2 "Robin", complete with logos, ready to enter service. *Photo: K. Gurney*

Right: As final preparations are made inside unit 17, an immaculate OV2 "Hurricane" awaits the first day of service. *Photo: E.L. Collinson*

A little drama occurred in the office when a heavy second-hand safe for holding small quantities of cash arrived, and nearly fell completely through the floor because of the very light construction of the building and its footings!

But, importantly, Bryan's masterplan had worked and with everything in place, it was simply a matter of waiting for the start date to come along. In the meantime, a company "get together" at OB was arranged, creating the opportunity for management and staff to bond in celebratory mood.

(Right picture): **Over wine and sandwiches, Neville Lobley (right), responsible for driver recruitment and training, chats with one of Bryan Constable's right hand men, Peter Hendy, now CBE and TfL's Commissioner.**

(Below): **Engineering appointments were overseen by Gerry May (right), pictured with a new recruit, against Roundabout's pristine fleet as backdrop.** *Photos: Austin Blackburn*

Hooray Hooray for Maroon & Grey!

Going Your Way

Marketing is the key to success for any new business. The 18-page "Going Your Way" booklet was the starting block for informing the public of their little new buses. The booklet was a vital tool to explain the changes, in some cases to win round folk, especially the concerned communities of St Pauls Cray estate. These residents disapproved of the changes, which replaced their familiar big red double deckers on route 229 in favour of 21 seat midibuses on route R1.

Never-the-less, the booklet promoted a great sense of excitement and an element of finesse in a fun style from cover to cover. The first seven pages were devoted to a written explanation of the changes due from 16th August 1986, using a novel approach. The front featured a cartoon of a fairground scenario, with a carousel carrying an RH and an OV full of passengers clearly enjoying their ride. The attraction is being acclaimed by an equally delighted audience, who are waving as the vehicles move round and round, picking up and dropping off riders.

The famous slogan "hooray hooray for maroon and grey" adorned the opening double page spread, featuring a series of small cartoon drawings. Most notably a jolly coachmaker was depicted in lively maroon and grey overalls, held up by his trusty braces, armed with a sturdy paintbrush in one hand and a tin of paint in the other. His sense of care and affection was conveyed as he proudly prepared his freshly turned out "nice little numbers in maroon and grey". In readiness to reach out to the community, the 21/25 seat buses were not so much going to paint the town red, rather to paint it maroon and grey!

Easy to Use

The booklet aimed to promote the positive aspects of the grand change. With experience gained from the GLC minibus experiments in 1972, the concept of "hail-and-ride" was introduced to Orpington. The ease and convenience of these small helpful buses stopping where passengers wanted them was highlighted.

Further slogans promised "the Roundabouts" will be friendly and frequent visitors down your way"; "Little and Often"; and "Their drivers will soon become fully fledged local characters". "Beating the town centre jam" was an important statement, illustrating the fact that these new "Roundabout" routes would serve the community on a purely local basis, and hence would not be vulnerable to the traffic congestion (Bromley by implication) causing companion trunk routes to suffer irregularity.

"Good holiday, Mrs Hirst?"

Friendly, satisfied cartoon caricatures throughout the booklet convey the notion that these messages are to be welcomed by all. A grandmother figure, wearing a bonnet with a maroon ribbon, featured in the carousel audience on the front cover, is identified in a further cartoon: a driver asks the grinning good lady "Good holiday, Mrs. Hirst?" as she boards his bus.

In line with Bryan's ambition to encourage positivity in the young, the same driver remarks "Congratulations on your exams, young Benny!" to a freckled schoolboy wearing school cap and tie. A pair of admiring young daughters gaze up at the driver of a passing bus as mum, sporting a 1960s "beehive" hairdo, appears to endorse cloth capped dad exclaiming "Hooray! A bus service that's right up our street!"

A passing bus on route R2 prompts young Benny to ask "Where's D2?", while a family group waves and calls "We're all for R4!" at a passing R4. Such was the expected focus on customer relations - frequent, friendly and reliable - that was the service Roundabout was to offer us.

Certainly the booklet succeeded in capturing the loyalty of one young boy back in 1986! The remainder of the booklet carried timetables for all the Roundabout routes, and the rear cover unfolded to show a map of the exciting new Orpington network.

Humble Beginnings

Most of the RH / OV fleet arrived in plenty of time at Unit 17, but rather than sit idly inside their home, they actively participated in a high profile publicity campaign. A number of "meet and greet" opportunities were advertised in the local press, organised at prominent venues such as the Walnuts shopping precinct and Orpington railway station, on the run up to the start of the new network. RH1 "Kestrel" and OV4 "Chinook" were shown off on a paved area of the Walnuts centre, attended by Roundabout and LRT staff handing out "Going Your Way" booklets and answering questions from curious passers-by. OV3 "Tornado" was positioned outside the Crofton exit from Orpington station one evening to capture the attention of homegoing commuters. In addition to this, on 1st August a photo call was arranged with a pair of Roundabout's finest on show, alongside vehicles from the other operators in the area also involved in the imminent change; namely Metrobus' sole Olympian of the time (C395DML), a red London Buses Leyland Titan, and a rather raggerty addition to this new 'impressive' line up in the form of an ex Glasgow Atlantean in LCBS green livery, ready for their take up of route 51. Leaflets were also available detailing the changes to other routes, which tended to be defined by the livery of the new operating companies, such as "Green Buses for route 51" and "Blue and Yellow Buses for Route 61".

These may have been humble beginnings for the Roundabout fleet, but before entering revenue earning service, the display buses provided the public with tangible evidence of the forthcoming revolution.

Above: Roundabout OV4, RH1, Metrobus 395, London Buses T818 and LCBS South East AN336 present at the colourful 1986 Press Launch at Orpington Station.
Photo: Graham Walker.

Below: how LRT presented the changes to the public, presenting an awareness of the liveries of the new operating companies: a montage extracted from the 16.8.86. timetable leaflets.

The new vehicles and their staff presented themselves to the public at the Walnuts centre in early August, when the "Going Your Way" booklet and timetable leaflets for the other altered services were distributed. *Photo: K. Gurney*

A Rising Star is Born

Whether it was "Here Comes a Rising Star" or "Going Your Way", the sell to the public was complete and Bryan and his team could do little more to promote their new enterprise. Roundabout would be under the spotlight as the frontrunner in the new approach to bus service provision. More importantly, Roundabout had the required number of staff, vehicles and an operating centre all in place well in time for the start date of 16th August.

The "Going Your Way" booklet featured this momentous image: the caricature prompts the author to ask: "is this a representation of Bryan Constable waving the flag at the start of an exciting new era in bus operations?"

43

Rather sadly, two OVs fell victim to callous acts of vandalism the night before their debut, and could not enter service on the day. RH8 "Swan" deputised for one OV on route R3, which was scheduled for exclusive OV operation. Although never proven, it was alleged that the vandalism was the work of a disgruntled LT employee from another garage. Thankfully this did not affect the morale of Roundabout staff.

On Saturday 16th August 1986, the first wheel to turn in revenue service for Roundabout belonged to one of the coach seated members of the RH fleet, which duly performed the 0543 route R1 departure from Foots Cray, only to be met by Bryan's son, who held the honour of being issued with the first Roundabout ticket number 001, as the first fare paying passenger. As the bus in its striking new livery progressed through Orpington, it became obvious that the maroon culture even extended to bus stops: "E" stickers in maroon were applied for any calling Roundabout route.

Orpington War Memorial was a popular location for bus enthusiasts, and many a ladder and long lens was noted recording the scene on the first day. Amongst the intended allocation of RH and OV to their designated routes, for added interest, enthusiasts would have noted the following:

- A1 working route R2;

- Coach seated RH1 "Kestrel" & RH24 "Seagull" on routes R1 & R5 respectively;

- RH8 "Swan" on route R3 deputising for a vandalised OV.

The driver of RH24 "Seagull" on route R5 calls in the "Rose & Crown" forecourt no doubt to exchange first day experiences with a colleague on OV3 "Tornado" *Photo: John Parkin*

YTS: keeping costs down!

As part of the "low cost unit" ideology, the office was staffed by a Youth Training Scheme student to assist with admin matters. Paul Bishop began on the Monday morning following the inauguration of Roundabout, and being a bus enthusiast himself and keen as mustard, he quickly became acquainted with garage operating practice and soon proved his usefulness to GM Peter Shulver. Paul was on day release to nearby Orpington College. He became the garage "go-for", but enjoyed assisting wherever he could. There was no photocopier at Unit 17, so Paul often had to go to Selkent HQ to use the machine there! At a later stage, HQ was moved to 68 Molesworth Street, Lewisham.

Trust in Staff

As the evening controller "shut up shop" at Unit 17, five duties would still be on the road. These drivers would be responsible for concluding their work unaided. On completion of their final trip, they would drive to the filling station, top up the tank with diesel by use of an ID vehicle fuelling card. They would then return to the garage and pay-in their takings by way of a "metal mickey" drop safe. The late turn engineer would be on hand to assist with vehicle defects, and ensure that sufficient buses were fit for the morning run-out.

We're All for R4; not so sure about R1

Although the Orpington 78222 switchboard recorded praise from Pauls Cray Hill residents delighted with their R4 service eliminating the long walk to catch route 51, many other calls from the other side of the River Cray were not so encouraging. Ken Glazier's maths were holding up, as complaints were received that passengers were being left behind after just a few stops along Midfield Way on route R1. Overcrowding resulted, as passengers felt squashed in the narrow gangwayed Robin Hoods, with nowhere to park shopping bags. A fresh look at LRT's specification for route R1 was required, and a solution was considered a high priority to avoid jeopardising the rest if the Roundabout operation which was doing so well.

Bromley Garage helps out on Route R5

The additional peak period capacity specified for route R5 was fulfilled by a red LS, running no. TB21. Dave Hales was regular driver on the evening peak turn, which formed the first half of Bromley garage duty 23. After dinner, the second half consisted of two rounders on route 227 TB9, and Dave considered this to be "the best duty in the garage!" Whilst working the R5, he soon built a positive rapport with the locals. Keeping an eye on train arrivals at Orpington Station, he would "adjust" his departure to ensure that his regular commuters were never left behind. Little wonder then that he joined OB to become a fully fledged Roundabout driver a few years later!

RH11 "Sparrow" pauses on the new markings of the Pauls Cray Hill terminus of the instantly popular hail and ride service, provided by route R4 for this community.
Photo: A. Jeffreys

Festive Spirits

Heavy snow descended on south-east England in December, yet the light purr of a ticking-over Iveco engine was a welcome sound on stand as the little bus waited patiently for custom. In these harsh operating conditions, a great deal of appreciation was demonstrated by passengers offering presents to the Roundabout drivers, whom they clearly felt had become a treasured feature of the locality. With four months' operating experience under their belt, Roundabout had justified itself and the rapport between staff and passengers had indeed materialised.

As 1987 dawned, Orpington Buses Ltd. had proved that services dedicated to local needs had lived up to expectations, and the sound quality of the name "Roundabout" was ready to build on success by expanding its coverage.

Boxing Day

On Boxing Day 1985, LRT had run a service over the whole of route 51, with a short working service over the Sidcup Station to Orpington Station section of route 229. For Boxing Day 1986, Roundabout was required to operate a service over the whole of route R1, but route 51 was withdrawn. As ever, route 208 operated Petts Wood – Lewisham.

1987

Patronage Up 10%; Improved Services

LRT published an interesting statistic during 1987. Following the average across the country, bus patronage was continuing to decline in London at around 2% per annum. However, it appeared that Orpington had bucked the trend, for a 10% *increase* in ridership had been recorded since the network revamp.

A1, bound for Green street Green on route R3, one of two red Dodges, picks up plenty of custom at the War Memorial stop in Orpington High Street on 8th December 1987. One year on from the inception of Roundabout, the Orpington network was clearly thriving. Photo: K. Gurney.

A number of improvements were introduced in response to this achievement, notably an increase in frequency from 30 to 20 minutes on route R4 from 31st October, and the introduction of a service on route R2 on Saturdays in the form of seven round trips. Double runs via Orpington Hospital were introduced also from 31st October on route R1 following requests from the public. A stop was positioned at the entrance to the new Canada Wing. These journeys ran 0830-2030 Monday to Friday, 1330-2030 Saturday and Sunday. Such bifurcations were generally applied to the Queen Marys Hospital – Green Street Green leg, although in the evenings, some Queen Marys Hospital – Bromley Common through journeys were scheduled via the hospital grounds. Regardless of origin / destination, all journeys running via Orpington Hospital carried the new route number R11.

Above: RH9 'Heron' on 14th November 1987 in Cray Avenue on its way into Orpington displaying the new route number R11, driven by Bert Cramer, a former SP driver.

Below: RH15 "Kingfisher" driven by another of Roundabout's venerable drivers, calls at the pond at Priory Gardens on 31st October 1987, heavily laden with St Pauls Cray estate passengers bound for Orpington. A notable feature of the bus stop is the red finial above the flag. *Photos: K.Gurney*

The rapid passenger growth added to the initial capacity difficulties being already being experienced on route R1. Bryan Constable admits to being embarrassed at this situation. Not a great company car user, Bryan would usually visit Roundabout by travelling to St Mary Cray by train and then catching an R1 (when there was room - more often there was not, in which case he trudged down the unkempt approach road, which uniquely featured a length of railway line as the kerb!) There were unquestionably insufficient seat-miles over the former 229 routeing via St Pauls Cray estate, especially for the 'short-hop' riders that the small buses were designed to target.

Behind the scenes LRT started to admit openly to bona fide pressure groups that it needed to address over-crowding on the R1, choosing to regard the overcrowding as a *downside of success* rather than a consequence of flawed mathematics as predicted by Ken Glazier! Unfortunately, LRT did not have the immediate financial ability to prematurely dispose of the very reliable RH family. The RHs had to be demonstrably needed elsewhere to create the consequential holes at Roundabout to enable bigger buses, in the form of stretched 33-seat Metroriders, to be secured for route R1. Almost as if by conjuring, the Bexleyheath plans, on the drawing board immediately after Roundabout started, found a need for partially written down, young very small buses: how incredibly convenient! Roundabout's 21 seat RHs fitted the bill! From November, RH 10 upwards were seconded to Bexleybus. As each RH departed to Eastbourne for repaint into their new biscuit and aircraft blue livery, standard length Metroriders already delivered for Bexleybus were progressively placed in service at OB, until Roundabout's own stretched Metroriders became available. For a few months, maroon and grey gave way to biscuit and blue on the streets of Orpington! The first ten MRLs arrived at OB in early January 1988, allowing their MR sisters to transfer to their intended shed just in time for the start of Bexleybus operations on 16th January.

R6: An Early Casualty

Developments in Kent had an early adverse impact on route R6. Green Line 706 (Victoria – Tunbridge Wells) succumbed to new Kentish Bus route 22 (Bromley – Badgers Mount – Halstead – Knockholt – Dunton Green – Tunbridge Wells), plus a new but infrequent (two round trips per weekday) route 21 (Orpington – Spur Road – Court Road – Polhill – Dunton Green – Bat & Ball – Sevenoaks). As a result of this increased Kentish Bus commercial activity between the North Downs villages and Sevenoaks, route R6 was withdrawn between Halstead and Sevenoaks from 30th May.

After just nine months, the maroon and grey livery was removed from the Kentish town of Sevenoaks, as seen here with OV4 "Chinook" on route R6 in the old Bligh's Meadow bus station on 16th August 1986. *Photo: John Parkin*

Boxing Day 1987

For the second year, a service was provided over route R1, with no service on route 51. Route 208 ran Petts Wood – Lewisham.

Fun 'n Games

During 1987, a number of amusing anecdotes surfaced, at least demonstrating there was room for a little harmless day-to-day "leg-pull". To assist with the smooth running of operations, each bus was equipped with a telephone supplied by Racal Vodafone, an early attempt at "mobile phones" (albeit with long curly flexes!). These were intended to be used between bus drivers and the garage control room; for example, a controller would simply dial "43" to reach "Puffin" or "54" to reach "Chinook". Some drivers used to a play a game whereby on seeing an oncoming Roundabout bus, they would flash the headlights to attract the approaching driver to stop, and immediately thrust the telephone with an extra-ordinary long flex out of the window to the passing driver, informing him/her that they had a telephone call, much to the bewilderment, then amusement of passengers taken in by this comical act! No doubt this is just one such escapade of many others as yet to be whispered out!

L.R.T. ROUTE **R6**

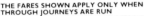

BUS PASSES, TRAVELCARDS AND CAPITALCARDS	
VALID IN ZONE	**ARE AVAILABLE BETWEEN**
OUTER 3 (ORANGE)	ORPINGTON I *and* KNOCKHOLT POUND 64

BUS PASSES, TRAVELCARDS AND CAPITALCARDS ARE NOT AVAILABLE FOR TRAVEL SOUTH OF KNOCKHOLT POUND

BETWEEN 0300 AND 0929 MONDAYS TO FRIDAYS (other than public holidays) all 30p fares above bold line are charged at

35p ◆

THE FARES SHOWN APPLY ONLY WHEN THROUGH JOURNEYS ARE RUN

CHILDREN

Up to two children under 5 years accompanying an adult or child ticket or pass holder and not occupying seats to the exclusion of other passengers are carried free

Children aged 5-15 years inclusive and additional children under 5 years, are charged the following fares for a single journey on one bus —

ABOVE LINE — from 0300 to 0929 hours Mondays to Fridays   20p
(except public holidays)
at other times   15p

BELOW LINE — half adult fare

CHILDREN AGED 14 AND 15 YEARS MUST BE IN POSSESSION OF A CHILD RATE PHOTOCARD EXCEPT LOCALLY BETWEEN STAGES 64 and 74.

TRAVEL PERMITS

Elderly and Handicapped Persons Travel Permits provided by the London Boroughs are available for free travel between Orpington (1) and Knockholt Pound (64) after 09.00 Mondays-Fridays and at any time Saturdays, Sundays and public holidays.

Kent Countywide Concessionary Bus Fare Permits allow travel at child fare (from 09.00 Mondays-Fridays where shown on permit) except locally between Orpington (1) and Chelsfield Bo Peep (6).

RETURN JOURNEYS

Except for journeys locally above the bold line, cheap day return fares are available after 09.00 Mondays-Fridays, and any time Saturdays, Sundays, public holidays in accordance with the following scale:—

SINGLE	RETURN
20	30
30	50
50	80
60	100
70	110
80	130
90	130
100	140
120	160

Return tickets and season tickets issued for LCB Route 706 are accepted for travel on this service.

Stage Point No.													
1	**ORPINGTON** *Station* 1												
2	30	**ORPINGTON** *War Memorial or Hillcrest Road* 2											
3	30	30	**ORPINGTON HOSPITAL** *(or SPUR ROAD Court Road)* 3										
4	30	30	30	**CHELSFIELD** *Station (or GODDINGTON LANE Shopping Parade)* 4									
5	**30**		30	**CHELSFIELD** *Five Bells* 5									
6			30	30	**CHELSFIELD** *Bo Peep* 6								
58			30	30	30	**HALSTEAD** *Watercroft Road* 58							
59				30	**BADGERS MOUNT** *Post Office* 59								
60	**30**	**30**		30	30	**ORPINGTON-BY-PASS** 60							
61				30	30	30	**HALSTEAD** *Clarks Lane or Cork* 61						
62				30	**SOUTHDENE** *Meadway* 62								
63	**30**	**30**	**30**	30	30	**PARK CORNER** 63							
64				30	30	30	**KNOCKHOLT POUND** *Three Horseshoes* 64						
65	50	50	50	50	50	50	50	50	30	30	20	**HAMPTON COTTAGES** 65	
66	80	80	80	80	80	80	80	80	70	70	50	30	**FOOT OF STAR HILL** *Keepers Cottage* 66
99	90	90	90	90	90	90	90	80	80	70	60	50	20	**SEVENOAKS-BY-PASS** 99
67	90	90	90	90	90	90	90	80	80	80	70	60	30	20	**DUNTON GREEN** *Rose and Crown* 67
68	90	90	90	90	90	90	90	90	90	80	80	70	50	30	20	**DUNTON GREEN** *LCB Garage or Station Road* 68
69	100	100	100	100	100	100	100	90	90	90	90	80	80	60	50	30	20	**LONGFORD** *Miners Arms* 69
70	100	100	100	100	100	100	100	100	100	90	90	80	80	60	50	30	30	20	**RIVERHEAD** *Homefield Road or Church* 70
71	120	120	120	120	120	120	120	100	100	100	100	90	90	70	60	50	50	30	20	**BRAESIDE AVENUE** 71
72	120	120	120	120	120	120	120	100	100	100	100	90	90	80	70	60	60	50	30	20	**SEVENOAKS** *Station* 72
73	**120**	**120**	**120**	120	100	100	100	90	80	70	60	60	50	30	30	20	**SEVENOAKS** *Vine* 73
74				120	120	100	100	100	80	80	70	70	60	50	30	20	20	**SEVENOAKS** *Bus Station* 74

(Rev. Jan. 87)

ROUNDABOUT R6

1987 FARE CHART: showing fare scales for cross-boundary route R6. The single fare from Orpington to Sevenoaks was the same as the 2010 Oyster fare for a single journey within Greater London. Roundabout drivers needed to be aware of the range of single and return fares available for out-county journeys, and the validity of season and return Green Line 706 tickets on route R6. By 2010, a rise around 600% seems to have occurred since the 1987 cash flat fare of 30p (35p in peaks)!

1988

A Bigger Home

The arrival of the stretched Metroriders during January indeed stretched the available space at OB, and thoughts turned to securing more spacious premises. Peter Shulver knew that just round the corner from Unit 17 at Nugent Estate a warehouse at Unit 5 lay empty, offering much more internal space plus better outside parking possibilities. Bryan Constable nodded the idea through, and Roundabout duly moved its operation to Unit 5. A set of FKI Bradbury Hi-wemer lifts was bought when the MRLs arrived.

Serving Tesco

Tesco opened a large "superstore" on a brownfield site along Edgington Way, a new road linking the Crittals Corner and Ruxley Corner roundabouts. From 16th July, a double run into the Tesco site during trading hours was introduced on route R1 / R11 journeys to/from Queen Marys Hospital 0830 – 2030 Mondays to Saturdays. The rule that journeys operating via Orpington Hospital should carry route number R11 held fast.

Goodbye R6, Hello R7

We saw in 1987 that Kentish Bus had increased its activities over the North Downs to the extent that route R6 had been withdrawn between Halstead and Sevenoaks. From 16th January 1988, Kentish Bus created a through Dartford – Swanley – Orpington – Sevenoaks corridor by extending their half-hourly route 17 (formerly 477) Joyce Green – Chelsfield southwards. Half the journeys were renumbered 18 and ran to Sevenoaks hourly via Polhill, Dunton Green and Bat & Ball, while route 17 worked hourly to Sevenoaks via Halstead, Knockholt and Dunton Green. These arrangements duplicated the remaining section of route R6, and the decision was taken to withdraw the route entirely from 26th March, thus depriving one member of the OV fleet of work. But not for long!

With three months left before complete withdrawal, route R6 finds Dodge A1 deputising for an OV on 23rd December 1987, depicted in Spur Road. The Dodges did not carry Roundabout logos, but in addition to LRT roundels, A1 retained the Swan logo, just visible to the right of the blind box, from its time with Leaside. *Photo: K. Gurney*

Kentish Bus route 18 operated over most of the remaining R6 route, resulting in withdrawal of the R6 from 26th March 1988. KB Atlantean 661 on route 18 bound for Sevenoaks loads in Orpington High Street, 30th December 1988. *Photo: K. Gurney*

Bryan and his team continued to look for opportunities to expand the small bus network, and took into account representations to serve the Coppice and Cockmannings Estates, both remote from existing bus services. These areas lay either side of Orpington, accessed by narrow roads; ideal territory for a new cross-Orpington midibus route. Thus route R7 was born on 16th July, with OV4 allocated, fittingly so as "Chinook" had been route bound on route R6! Route R7 ran hourly during Monday to Saturday shopping hours, from a new stand in Waldenhurst Road into Orpington High Street. After circumnavigating the War Memorial, buses ran via the steeply graded Knoll Rise, then Mayfield Avenue and St Johns Road, taking the opportunity to serve further areas unserved by bus. Route R7 became the first to operate under the Tudor Way low bridge, then ran via Petts Wood and into the Coppice Estate. A loop of the estate was performed without standing, before retracing the entire route back to Cockmannings.

OV4 'Chinook' is seen in Petts Wood on the first journey on the first day of route R7, having collected a full load of happy pensioners from the Coppice Estate. Pat Carter is at the wheel, with a very young Paul Bishop observing.

All manner of OB vehicles appeared on this single bus allocation, including RHs, demonstrators and loans such as Talbot Pullman E630 MAC, and Metroriders such as MRL 77, the last to enter the Roundabout fleet.
Photos: K. Gurney

A further change to the route R5 arrangements also occurred from 16th July. Bromley garage's peak period LS operation over route R5 was replaced by a Roundabout RH, which between 1555 and 1805, did not carry passengers locally between Orpington and Green Street Green. By way of support over this local leg, the LS was redeployed, reinstating the former route number 471, to run at 20 minute "with flow" headway in the morning and evening peaks.

TB driver "Bruno" negotiates the narrow country lanes in LS 406. Bromley's involvement in assiting Roundabout became less needed on route R5, and was changed soon after to support just the Green Street Green – Orpington corridor as route 471.

Although route R6 had been withdrawn and its journeys transferred to route R5, the unofficial use of "R5A" was often shown to indicate journeys operating via Badgers Mount. OV5 "Whirlwind" showing "R5A" sits in the sun at Orpington Station. *Photos: A. Jeffreys*

Boxing Day 1988

For Boxing Day, Monday 26th December 1988, LRT decided the R11 routeing via Orpington Hospital should operate, and a half-hourly service over the whole line of route ran 1200 – 2000. Again route 51 did not run, and route 208 operated Petts Wood – Lewisham.

1989: Seeing red!

Peter Shulver accepted promotion as General Manager of Dial-a-Ride, and in June, Adrian Jones took over the General Manager post at Roundabout.

Until 1989, major maintenance issues had been largely being dealt with under manufacturers' warranty. As the fleet aged, an engineering team of six evolved to continue maintenance cover. Austin Blackburn, Selkent's Technical Assistant, was seconded from Headquarters (68 Molesworth Street, SE13) to become Workshop Foreman, leading four shift engineers and an assistant engineer. Unit 5 now felt sufficiently competent and confident to undertake *any* maintenance involving the RH / OV / MRL fleet, indeed performing tasks such as engine, gearbox and axle rebuilds, interior refurbishments and full resprays, much of which bigger garages would outsource. Austin's secondment was only intended to last six months, but the team earned a reputation for dedication in tending this small, well kept fleet, and having given up the office in favour of "going back to the tools", he stayed in this capacity until privatisation!

Preparations for FFD (Freedom From Defect) certification required chasses and engines to be steam cleaned of road silt. For this purpose, until 1989, members of the fleet could be seen trundling through Eynsford village to the steam cleaning facility at the small Home Farm industrial estate. Here, the process would be witnessed by shaggy, ginger coloured Highland cattle in the field behind, against the backdrop of the Victorian architecture of the railway viaduct spanning the River Darenth. From 1989, the purpose-built Mark-Kelly Coachworks steam cleaning ramp at the less rustic venue of Jason's Tours Green Street Green workshop was utilised by Roundabout. After MoT preparations, buses were sent to New Cross for testing, although at a later date, vehicles went to the Purfleet test centre.

Meanwhile, at 55 Broadway, the London Buses (LBL) Design Director, Jeremy Rewse-Davies, considered that London Buses' image needed redefining, to reinforce the fact that the "low cost" units Roundabout, Bexleybus and Harrow Bus were very much integral constituents under the corporate umbrella. He felt that these colourful subsidiaries needed to be perceived by the public as part of London's unified network.

Furthermore, the trades unions were becoming increasingly fearful that management appeared to be distancing itself from the superior remuneration packages negotiated for staff at other garages. LBL felt that application of its corporate red livery to the low cost unit fleets would demonstrate a unified image to the public, and suppress union anxiety. So maroon and grey, aircraft blue and biscuit, and red and cream were to be consigned to the history books.

The first change was simply that some of the OV/MRL received small "SELKENT" fleetnames complete with the hops logo, suitably applied on their maroon/grey livery, but that was only the start of what would become a big image change for Roundabout. Within a few months Adrian was to oversee the Roundabout fleet pass into corporate LBL red livery, complete with grey skirts and white bands, although the livery scheme stopped short of the application of yellow doors, nor did the London Buses roundel feature. Instead, doors remained red while large "ROUNDABOUT" logos continued to adorn either side of the vehicles.

An early indication of change as seen here on 19th August 1989 was "Kingfisher II" displaying a small Selkent logo strap, complementing the established maroon & grey livery. Unusually allocated to route R5, what was to become MRL 69 is passing the since demolished Orpington Village hall. *Photo: K. Gurney*

The first Roundabout bus to go red was actually OV3 in October, and in doing so lost it's 'Tornado' pet name, to be followed by OV1 'Typhoon' in December. However, this marked the commencement of a scheme to replace the troublesome manual gearbox original City Pacers, for OV1 and OV3 never returned to Roundabout service after repaint, but were sent to Plumstead (PD) to join the training bus fleet there. Their automatic gearbox replacements, OV44 and OV49, already in red livery, arrived at OB from Victoria's basement garage (GB) and so became semi-permanent additions to the Roundabout fleet. The same shed also parted with OV26 and 38, plus the two blue liveried Chelsea Hopper Iveco Dailys, RH19 and 22, which therefore joined their siblings at OB over three years late! RH19 was painted into corporate red livery before leaving Victoria, while RH22 was similarly treated at Plumstead.

RH19 was a new addition to the Roundabout fleet seen in Franks Wood Avenue on route R7, having spent life so far in other liveries at Eastbourne and Chelsea. On 6th November 1989, RH19 was sporting LBL red, white band and grey skirts, but was still awaiting decals. *Photo: K. Gurney*

RH5 'Owl' and RH6 'Swift' were repainted at OB over Christmas 1989, becoming the first of the original fleet members to be so treated with the intention of staying in service at Roundabout.

Despite Roundabout losing its highly admired colourful identity, the process did gain something that Bryan was not granted clearance upon three years previously. Appearance of the garage code, OB (Orpington Buses) could now be displayed proud of place on each vehicle!

For those at the sharp end, to help drivers make sense of it all, a red holdall was issued, emblazoned with symbols representing the total Selkent operation, including the "hops" logo, the titles "Bexleybus", "Roundabout", "Selkent" and "Selkent Travel", and the words "London's Red Buses".

The plum coloured Roundabout jumper, jacket and tie were no longer issued, replaced with navy blue jumper, blazer and tie, with red "Selkent" and hops logos. In common with the rest of the Selkent fleet, Roundabout's drivers became protected by assault screens – a necessary sign of the times – and the Racal Vodafones were replaced by the standard Band III radio equipment.

Roadworks Afflict Route R4

From 12th June, long term roadworks in Tubbenden Lane sent route R4 on a lengthy diversion between Orpington and Locks Bottom. Buses were diverted off Tubbenden Lane to run via Southcroft Road, Ridgeway Crescent, Leamington Avenue, Borkwood Way, Northlands Avenue, Oakleigh Gardens, Sevenoaks Road, Farnborough Hill, and Farnborough by-Pass to Starts Hill Road. This diversion was performed in service, and eventually became popular, and elements of it were incorporated into a service proposal some eighteen months later.

However, just to rub salt into the wound, in December, further roadworks afflicted the Orpington – Pauls Cray Hill end of the route, and buses diverted via Sevenoaks Way. It became impossible to operate the scheduled 20 minute headway, and reluctantly, a temporary half-hourly service was imposed for the next fifteen months.

Meeting Requests

Once again, Bryan's team responded to local requests for improvements to services, with a small package of alterations from 21st October.

An earlier arrival in Orpington from Biggin Hill was achieved with an additional journey on route R2 at 0729-ex Biggin Hill Valley Monday-Friday (0754 Saturday).

Morning positioning runs to Petts Wood on route R3 were livened-up on reaching Poverest Road, to provide one earlier and two additional morning peak arrivals to meet London commuter trains at Petts Wood station. To accommodate requests for a later R3 bus from Petts Wood station, an R1 journey terminating at Bromley Common had a live section introduced into its otherwise dead run to OB; it operated via Petts Wood station to meet the 2338 ex-Charing Cross train (very popular Friday and Saturday nights), thence working in service as the 0010 R3 to Cray Avenue, before finishing at OB.

The single vehicle allocated to shopping hours only route R7 was given Monday to Friday peak period work, when it would shuttle between Petts Wood station and the Coppice Estate at 20 minute intervals, matching the rail service cycle.

On 24th June 1992, RH4 "Dove" with Mitzy, a regular driver, is seen in the evening peak operating the R7 shuttle. *Photo: K. Gurney*

The Renault Trial

For the spring and summer, Roundabout was host to a 31 seat Northern Counties bodied Renault S75 (with a Perkins engine) in a refreshing light blue and cream colour scheme for Preston Bus. This vehicle experienced several mishaps during its stay, for example, finding itself on Sidcup Hill running over its own battery set which had slid out of its tray! The alternator was unreliable, leading to a notorious episode as recalled by Austin Blackburn, who was called out to Sandown Park racecourse after the Renault failed to start up for the return leg of a private hire, driven by Roy Sewell.

Visiting NC / Renault midibus on route R1 in Perry hall Road, 24th June 1989, having passed the 208 stand, where LS 382 awaits its next journey amongst the play of a Saturday's allocation of Titans. *Photo: K. Gurney*

Colourful Visitors

Above: Sherpa F419 BOP arrives at Petts Wood Station Square on route R3, 1st September 1989, clearly showing the two company addresses on the nearside skirting panel: 1) Carlyle Bus Works: 2) Selkent. *Below:* Busways no. 1121 on hire from Carlyle, was able to accommodate correct blinds within its display area, seen on route R1 in Orpington High Street, 23rd October 1989. *Photos: K. Gurney*

Throughout 1989 there was a proliferation of visiting midibuses to the Orpington scene, bringing with them a colourful mix of liveries. The Carlyle bus works loaned several Sherpas with manual transmission to Roundabout as vehicle cover whilst some of OB's regulars were sent to address difficulties at Bexleybus. The host of liveries was displayed across all the "R" routes, and incompatible blind fittings necessitated the frequent use of "cornflake box and felt-tip marker pens" to display route and destination information.

After such a colourful performance in Orpington, once matters stabilised at Bexleybus, Roundabout vehicles returned home, and the Sherpas went off-hire back to Carlyle at Edgbaston.

Martin Edwards at the wheel of this cream liveried Sherpa from Carlyle Bus Works. E968 SVP on route R11 rounds Orpington War Memorial on 19th August 1989.

Photo: K. Gurney

Boxing Day 1989

For Tuesday 26th December, LRT reinstated route 51 over its full Woolwich – Orpington line of route, but at the expense of route R11, which meant that Roundabout had no operational work on Boxing Day 1989. Route 208 again operated Petts Wood – Lewisham.

1990

The year started with a competition to find "Britain's Brightest Bus Service". The Roundabout team was entered, and Centrewest fielded their route E5; however, the honour was bestowed on Grey Green for their route 24.

Fleet Changes

Heavy passenger loadings on routes R1 / R11 began taking its toll on MRL rear suspension mountings, and the quest for an even more robust vehicle resulted in the choice of Carlyle bodied Denis Darts (DTs) for deployment on these busy routes. Thirteen Darts (DT28-41) began replacing the MRLs from 9th June, however, the Darts were prone to grounding at the junction of Orpington Hospital approach road and Sevenoaks Road, located just behind MRL73 in the picture opposite.

A number of MRLs were retained for use on route R11, but from 9th June, any Dart operated R11 journey omitted the hospital double run. From 14th July until 15th August, route R11 was entirely withdrawn from the hospital grounds whilst roadworks were carried out to alleviate the grounding problem.

From August, Carlyle bodied Mercedes 811D (MC2-5) began replacing the quartet of automatic transmission OVs. A little triumph for Bryan here, as the LRT favoured OV was ousted by the latest version of Bryan's original "Rising Star" choice of Mercedes midibus! The MC class introduced "red diamond" seating moquette to Roundabout.

RH8 "Swan", often mistakenly called "Susan" due to the appearance of the scrolled "Palace Script" decals, spent the summer at BX to cover Bexleybus' repaint programme into corporate red.

During 1990, OB was host to a couple of visitors. Blue/silver Metrorider G689KNW stayed a while in May, being a demonstrator from Optare following purchase of the jigs, tooling and rights after the demise of Metro Camell Weymann (MCW) a year earlier. In November, MTL3 (H189RWF), a Reeves Burgess bodied Mercedes 811D, appeared on Roundabout routes before transfer to Catford garage.

Above: Optare's Metrorider demonstrator on loan to Roundabout turns into Carlton Parade on route R1, full to capacity plus standing on 10 April 1990.

Below: Stages in MRL manufacture at Optare's Crossgates factory. *Photos: K. Gurney*

A very wet Station Square, Petts Wood, sees MRL145 on route R3 at rest with its large windscreen wipers stopped at an intermediate point in their travel. **New Year's Eve 1990.** *Photo: K. Gurney*

Festive Season

In December, MC 2-5 were called upon to operate a special set of festive shoppers' specials, "Centrelink", from Catford garage. By way of cover, a batch of brand new Optare Metroriders, MRL 142-5, intended for Plumstead garage's route 380, were temporarily drafted to OB for route R3.

For a second year, LRT decided not to operate a service over route R11 on Boxing Day, Wednesday 26th December. However, special one-day contracts were awarded to Boroline to operate route 51, and to Metrobus to operate route 208 between Orpington (for the first time) and Catford.

1991

Red Noses

Although Roundabout could look forward to its fifth birthday in August, the year 1991 started badly for Selkent. Tender results for the Woolwich / Bexleyheath area resulted in the demise of Bexleybus. Amongst the disposals, RH15 was "rescued" and reunited with her sisters at Roundabout to satisfy a pvr increase on route R4, and her former pet name "Kingfisher" was applied in February.

Bromley Council delivered the next bout of unwelcome news, when it proposed various traffic calming measures in Knoll Rise, including closure to through traffic and/or installation of "sleeping policemen". Despite representations pointing out the impact on bus route R7, Knoll Rise was closed to through traffic for a trial period of eight weeks from 29th September. Route R7 was diverted from Knoll Rise via Lucerne Road, St Kilda Road, Beswick Road and Broomhill Road (towards Cockmannings) or White Hart Road (towards Coppice). It proved impossible to complete the round trip in 60 minutes, so a temporary timetable featuring an 80 minute headway was imposed. Eighteen months later, the council decided upon the road hump option, whereupon route R7 was withdrawn permanently from Knoll Rise; by then, tenure of route R7 had fallen to Kentish Bus.

However, other sets of intrusive roadworks were completed in early 1991, and a 20 minute headway was restored to route R4. Elements of the diversion off Tubbenden Lane had proved popular, and from 21st April, the R4 was rerouted away from a 400 metre section of Tubbenden Lane to operate via Tubbenden Drive, Northlands Avenue, Southlands Avenue and Beechcroft Lane.

The "Comic Relief" charity campaign lifted spirits a little, as Roundabout staff adorned most buses in their fleet with a large "red nose". With some ingenuity, it was demonstrated that a red nose could be secured even to the front of a Carlyle Dart!

RH1 "Kestrel" in a fresh coat of red paint, complete with "Comic Relief" red nose, passes through Green Street Green on route R5, 28th March 1991. *Photo: Julian Smith*

A duo of red noses with MC5 on route R3 driven by Joseph Udomhiaye approaching Orpington War Memorial and RH19 on route R4 chasing. 28th March 1991. *Photo: Julian Smith*

On close inspection, it can be seen that DT32 has been fitted with red nose, passing the cheerful fruit seller, sadly no longer a feature of Orpington's High Street scene. *Photo: Julian Smith*

At the end of March, Orpington was yet again selected for bedding-in another new vehicle for Catford garage (TL), in the shape of the Dennis Wright Handybus. DW59 appeared for four weeks working routes R3 and R11, bringing an Ulster registration plate (JDZ2359) to Orpington.

The Rose & Crown forecourt at Green Street Green was for very many years a bus terminating facility, typified on 13th April 1991 with two Dart variants resting between journeys. The Wright bodied DW59 was a visitor to OB, seen on route R3, alongside resident Carlyle bodied DT32 (still with red nose!) on route R11. Like many landlords of former coaching inns, a later licencee decided to end the traditional bus terminating practice, and buses now stand in the road, rather obstructively, opposite the oast house conversion visible in the background. *Photo: K. Gurney*

In April, MC1 moved from TL to OB to join MC2-5 as the spare vehicle for the R3 allocation. MC1 had her "Catford Cat" motifs removed before entering in service. DT41 moved from OB to TB to make space for the new arrival.

In the summer, Bromley garage was disposing of its Darts to London United, but in June, coach seated DT55 was sent to OB, which parted with DT29 to Fulwell in 'payment' for not receiving DT55.

Happy 5th Birthday

All five original named Optare City Pacers had been painted in corporate red livery with a view to joining Plumstead's training fleet. However, OV2 was returned to OB after a matter of months, and had languished at the back of the shed. Bryan Constable decided that OV2 should feature in Roundabout's modest fifth birthday celebrations, and had the vehicle restored to maroon and grey livery complete with her name "Hurricane". With a splendid restoration project completed in good time, Bryan felt that a 5th Birthday reunion of the original "Rising Star" team would be appropriate. On a sunny summer afternoon, Austin Blackburn drove OV2 with Bryan Constable, Peter Hendy and Bob Muir aboard to the picturesque location of Chevening for a picnic lunch and a photoshoot.

OV2 "Hurricane" posed in Chevening while the "Rising Star" team admire a fine piece of restoration! *Photo: B. Constable*

OV2 then was placed on show at Plumstead garage's Open Day, in company with other exhibits from the immaculate Selkent Travel fleet. In a magnanimous gesture, Bryan formally donated "Hurricane" to the London Transport Museum. However, on 17th August, David Hulls drove OV2 to the Walnuts centre just one more time. With the assistance of a member of Selkent Travel staff, "Hurricane" formed a small commemorative display, which included copies of the original "Going Your Way" booklet for the benefit of passers-by.

Happy birthday — five years on

ROUNDABOUT celebrated its fifth birthday on 16 August.

In 1986, London Buses set up a subsidiary company — Orpington Buses Limited — in a successful bid to win a new network of midibus routes in and around the Orpington area, offered to competitive tender by London Transport.

Always run under the distinctive ROUNDABOUT fleet name, the operation — with its base at St Mary Cray — became part of Selkent in 1989.

To mark the fifth birthday, one of the first Roundabout buses — OV2, an Optare City Pacer — was restored to its original maroon and grey livery.

OV2 was presented to the London Transport Museum during Selkent's Open Day at

OV2 before its presentation to the London Transport Museum

Plumstead garage in July.

It had an outing to Orpington on 17 August, when it formed the centrepiece of a display tracing the story of Roundabout's first five years, held at the Walnuts Shopping Centre.

Extract from "LT News"

Boxing Day 1991

LRT tried a novel approach to Orpington's Boxing Day bus service provision for 1991. Neither route 51 nor 208 ran; instead, a half-hourly service on route R11 was operated by Roundabout, extended to Bromley North for connection into route 47 (Bromley South – Shoreditch). Notably, this was the one and only occasion when an "R"-prefix route was scheduled to Bromley town centre.

1992: Hoppa is a dirty word

Hops were fine, taking pride of place as the logo with the Selkent name, but "Hoppas" were not so fine! "Hoppa" was the brand name to be seen on the streets of many a provincial city, and catching on fast in the late 1980s London bus scene. "Harrow Hoppa", "Walthamstow Hoppa" and even "Central Hoppa": the list went on as the "Hoppa" logo was applied almost routinely to the sides of London Buses' Metroriders, Starriders, et al. Despite the term being synonymous with a localised small bus network, "Hoppa" was not for the likes of Roundabout!

Being the unique gem that it was, Roundabout bucked the trend and declined to carry such labelling, for Bryan Constable felt strongly that the term "Hoppa" was degrading, and conveyed a cheap and tacky image of bus transportation.

In May 1992, the ubiquitous Selkent midibus floats, MR14/35/38/51, were doing the rounds switching and swapping their way around the four garages (TB/TL/PD and OB). They came to Selkent after being made redundant from the Westlink and Harrow midibus schemes, still wearing the ever ready large 'Hoppa' stickers. MR14 proved an excellent candidate fulfilling a need for a Bellingham – Catford Bridge shuttle route 138A, as a result of tree lopping affecting route 138 for about a month. But the unplanned arrival of MR14 at OB joined one of the rare occasions "Hoppa" branding would briefly meet the eyes of Orpingtonians. Despite so short a stay, MR14 soon become dressed with a full set of *"ROUNDABOUT"* logos, and the disgraced "Hoppa" logos were removed and no doubt ripped up with all haste!

Harking back to Orpington High Street 16th November 1989, MBV46 arrived at OB wearing the dreaded "Hoppa" insignia! Like MR14, this offending slogan was very quickly replaced with "Roundabout" decals.
Photo: K. Gurney

MR14 brought to Roundabout a further example of "red diamond" seating moquette, although a little jaded since its Westlink days from new at Hounslow, and became a regular initially on route R4, then new route R8.

MR14 on R7 on the West Approach stand, Petts Wood station, during the last months of the route with Roundabout. *Photo: K.Gurney*

The original number one of the OB fleet, RH1 "Kestrel", was repainted back into maroon and grey Roundabout livery and entered service initially devoid of logos or fleet numbers. On route R5 in Spring 1992 on the turning circle at Orpington Station. *Photo: Graham Walker*

In the days when publicity for route changes were more prolific, the public enjoyed household drops of leaflets such as these for the 1992 package.

Changes to the Network (a route lost & a route gained!)

By July, LRT unveiled plans for further improvements to the Orpington network. Having since 1986 improved services in St Pauls Cray and St Mary Cray villages, and the vast St Pauls Cray municipal estate, attention was turned to the smaller St Mary Cray municipal estates either side of Blacksmith Lane. Kentish Bus 476/477/478 double deck group operated via Blacksmith Lane en route between Orpington and Crockenhill, however, LRT felt it was possible to extend the midibus ideology to serve the narrow estate roads. Furthermore, it was thought that the Coppice Estate service could be improved to operate every 20 minutes throughout the day.

An extensive revision to route R7 was proposed, however, the work was awarded to Kentish Bus, using Metroriders from Dartford (DT) garage. Petts Wood station, West Approach, was to be the terminal, from where buses would follow the existing R7 routeing via Coppice estate, but then ran via Chesham Avenue and Shepperton Road to reach Tudor Way, thence St Johns Road and Knoll Rise into Orpington. After Orpington High Street, route R7 would be diverted away from Cockmannings, operating instead via routes 476/477/478 to St Mary Cray village. Loops via the Sandway estate and Burfield Drive would be performed, with two out of three buses per hour returning via the reverse outward routeing to Petts Wood. The remaining one bus per hour would continue via the 477 routeing through Crockenhill, Swanley, Hextable and Wilmington to Dartford.

Cockmannings was to receive a new hourly midibus route R8, which would run across Orpington and on to Chelsfield village via route 477. Happily, the R8 was awarded to Roundabout when the package was introduced from 21st November. It was therefore possible to withdraw the 476/477/478 group from Greater London, ending the sight of double deckers performing the branch covered narrow-laned Chelsfield loop!

MR14 making gentle progress through Chelsfield's country lanes on the new route R8 in summer 1993. *Photo: Graham Walker*

RH1 at the former R7 Cockmannings terminus on the first day of new route R8, 21st November 1992. *Photo: K. Gurney*

Route R8 operated Monday to Saturday only, thus depriving Chelsfield village of the Sunday service provided by route 477.

The arrangements also swept away the Sunday practice of extending route 477 beyond the Hewitt's roundabout along the A21 to Pratts Bottom, thence to provide a Sunday service over route 402 into Bromley. The unique fast thrash along dual carriageways on the top of a double decker (often a Kentish Bus Scania) was sorely missed by some young enthusiasts! As part of the package, route 402 was reintroduced every two hours Bromley – Pratts Bottom, interworked every two hours with route 320 Bromley – Biggin Hill.

A wet Sunday afternoon brings a Scania to route 477 seen at Orpington Memorial en route from Bromley North to Swanley.
Photo: K. Gurney

75

LRT did not require a service on route R7 between Orpington and Petts Wood in the evenings or on Sundays. At these times, Kentish Bus operated hourly from Orpington to Dartford. If a journey operated via Hextable, it carried route number R7 throughout; however, some journeys operated via Joydens Wood, changing blinds once clear of the Greater London boundary to show "R76".

The 21st November package brought many further alterations to Roundabout's routes. An extension to hourly route R2 was introduced, by paralleling route R3 from Orpington to Petts Wood, but diverting off Poverest Road via Austin Road, Sidmouth Road, Amherst Drive, Dorney Rose, Sherborne Road and Church Hill Wood.

From Saturday 21st November 1992
New service for Tillingbourne Green on Route R2. More buses for Halstead. Change of bus colour on the R7: better service for Coppice Estate and Sandway Road . New Route R8 to serve Cockmannings Estate and Chelsfield. Metrobus 358 to serve Bromley Town Centre . R3 to serve shops at Green Street Green and have an evening service. For further details ☎ 071-222 1234 at any time.

On route R1, journeys via Orpington Hospital were introduced from 0830 on Saturdays, thus conforming to the Monday to Friday period of operation, and carried "R11" as appropriate. Routes R1 and R11 also incorporated double runs to serve Tescos on Sundays during trading hours 1000-1600.

ORPINGTON BUS NETWORK

All journeys on route R3 operated via Orpington Station irrespective of direction or time of day, and were extended to Green Street Green, where the terminating arrangements for route R3 were amended. A live one-way loop, incorporating two minutes stand time at the Queens Head, was introduced from Windsor Drive, via Glentrammon Road, High Street, Vine Road and World's End Lane.

To meet requests following a rail timetable change, the late night 0012 R3 from Petts Wood to Cray Avenue was retimed to 0030.

A double run was introduced from Knockholt to Halstead on all route R5 journeys. The use of route number R6 was reinstated, to denote those circular peak journeys which route R5 operated via Badgers Mount. However, route 471, which supplemented route R5 between Green Street Green and Orpington station on a "with flow" peak basis, was withdrawn, following a bold commercial move by Metrobus. Route 358 had operated Orpington – Crystal Palace, routeing direct via Crofton Road to Locks Bottom. Metrobus rerouted their service via Green Street Green and Farnborough, essentially reversing the 1986 change by reintroducing the severed route 261 links! Of course Green Street Green and Farnborough residents were highly delighted with their reinstated frequent service to Bromley. Route 361 was now redundant, and was withdrawn from 21st November. The writing was also on the wall for routes R1/R11 between Green Street Green and Bromley Common, but these routes remained intact into CentreWest days.

Left: **Keen to observe the new changes, local resident and ODRPA Chairman David Daters beside RH2 'Robin' on the first day of the extended R2 at Petts Wood. RH2 was one of a small number fitted with fog lights to assist in the narrow Downe lanes.**
Photo: K.Gurney

Boxing Day:

LRT continued to exhibit a taste for unusual routeings and special one day contracts in 1992. No service operated on routes R11, 51 or 208. A hybrid route 211 embraced elements of these routes, running from Queen Mary's Hospital via route R11 to Orpington, thence via route 208 to Bromley North. The contract was awarded to Metrobus.

1993

Star Attraction

With the RH fleet approaching its seventh birthday, thought was given to a likely successor. Ten Ford Marshall 23 seat Ivecos were decided upon, and duly delivered in April. They were shown off to the press in a line up at the LT Sports and Social Club at Langley Park on 25th April 1993.

FMs being presented to the press at Langley Park . A unique opportunity to meet Roundabout drivers was a great bonus. *Photos: K. Gurney*

FM1 on arrival at Jubilee Country Park prior to the 31st July naming ceremony. This side profile displays the welcoming step lights leading to the red diamond moquette interior. *Photo: R.T.Fickling*

Soon after the FMs entered service, the author wrote, at the age of ten, to Bryan to ask if the buses could have pet names, as the MC and DT did not have them. Therefore when the RHs were retired, the practice of naming would die out. If this were allowed to happen, the author felt Roundabout would lose the special identity in the community so treasured in the early days. For the FM class, he suggested signs of the zodiac.

Bryan expressed delight with the idea and was keen for an official naming ceremony. This certainly was a great example of encouragement towards young people and was a real uplift in terms of childhood spirits for the author.

On 31st July, FM1 was brought to Jubilee Park for the purpose of unveiling the name of the first star sign of the year, "Capricorn" (although the author had a secret yearn for it to be named "Gemini" after his own star sign!)

Photo: K. Gurney   **79**

Family and some school friends together with local passengers and neighbours were in attendance together with the local Press, and the ceremony was followed by a buffet at the nearby scout hall. The author's father, at the time a member of the London Regional Passengers' Committee, took the opportunity to make a speech in praise of the achievements of Roundabout, and prophetically as it turned out, cautioned those in charge of the tendering process not to be influenced by cheap bids, but to have regard for proven ability to deliver a quality, responsive bus service.

For the record, the author's star sign was allocated to FM6! FM7 was sequentially named "Cancer", but in view of the unpleasant connotations associated with this name, after a few days it was rechristened "Scorpio". The remaining twelfth name, "Sagittarius", was never used, although rumour suggested that BL85 was to receive the name; in the event this never happened. It was later learned that the transfers applied to the FMs had been ordered privately by Bryan, who paid £50 out of his own pocket!

FM3 "Pisces" on route R3 deputising for an MC. Passing Orpington Post Office, the Watson & Gurney vehicle in pursuit is of no known connection with the author's family! 14th March 1994. *Photo: G. Walker*

Enter BL 85

With arrival of the FM class, Roundabout boasted a relatively modern fleet, and the need for extensive vehicle maintenance reduced somewhat, with the consequence that OB's workshop workforce was reduced by one. However, the need to refurbish the MC class was identified, and Marshalls of Cambridge agreed to part fund the programme. The idea of deploying a "big" bus took hold to cover the allocations shortfall. In the autumn of 1993, Roy Sewell took a Leyland National on trials over routes R1/R3/R11. However the LS became stranded in the grounds of Orpington Hospital testing the R11 route, and so it never came....

The need to look elsewhere for a full size single deck bus that would be a cheap temporary addition to the fleet resulted in an unusual visitor coming to lodge with Roundabout in the shape of a 1976 Bristol LH. Workshop Foreman Austin Blackburn was given the task of inspecting and selecting such a vehicle from London United, which had three BL trainers for disposal. Out of BL80/85/86 parked-up at Shepherds Bush garage, Austin considered that BL85 be selected.

Without the large rear overhang of the LS, and slightly narrower body, the choice of BL85 at a mere 7ft 6ins wide, proved ideal. This type of 39 seater vehicle last served the Bromley area in the early 1980s on routes B1/146 from Bromley garage (TB) although this particular example was not from this area, and had been a training bus at Shepherds Bush (S) for many years. BL85 re-entered PSV service, on 3rd December 1993 on route R4 as OB43, freshly painted in red, sporting a white band below the windows with grey skirt, a full set of front/side/rear blinds, and of course large "ROUNDABOUT" logos! In theory, BL85 was to be used on the R1/R11, to release a DT to the R3, but the BL could be seen on the R1/R3/R4/R8/R11 if the driver felt up to the task, even relishing the challenge and opportunity of driving a bigger bus over their usual route.

BL85 sported black and white metal registration plates OJD85R, together with the blue and silver sprayed 'BRISTOL LH' badge on the radiator grill. Such features were a delight for local enthusiasts; the author recalls having enjoyed a ride one evening on the R1 in the rain, with the distinctive sound of the wiper motors thrashing the rain off the windscreen; not forgetting the yellow "washing line" – which formed the interior bell cord!

Due to a change in licencing laws, drivers who had initially passed as a class3 manual PSV (midibus test) could drive **any** PCV vehicle. There were mixed views from drivers on having what was technically a "big" bus at their garage. Some really enjoyed driving such a gentle beast, as her gear changes gave way to a delightful "chirp" sound. Drivers holding affection for BL85 in particular were Bert Cramer on his regular morning R8 duty, and Barry Philpott on his afternoon R4 duty. However, drivers were given the option of substituting BL85 on their intended duty.

Above: BL85 at the R1 Grovelands Road stand, 9th May 1994. *Photo: G. Walker.*
Below: The influx of FMs still left a requirement for five RHs of which RH3 "Puffin" was one, subsequently fitted with a Dart one-piece route number blind, seen passing "Safeway" (now "Morrisions") Petts Wood 21st August 1992, three months before route R7 was lost to Kentish Bus. *Photo: K. Gurney*

As the MC refurbishment program commenced, FM3 needed accident repairs at Marshalls. Therefore an additional replacement bus, in the shape of West Midlands Travel Metrorider 632 (D632NOE) from Perry Barr depot, was lent to OB, until February 1994.

Reminiscent of OV4's problems on page 154 in 1989, FM1 similarly expired at the same location in the hot summer of 1994, with watering cans for comfort and MC1 & 5 for company. *Photos: Tom Gurney*

Route Losses

Bad news rounded off 1993, as Roundabout suffered further losses to Kentish Bus. From 4th December, following retendering, routes R5 and R6 transferred to Dunton Green garage.

Boxing Day

Once again, for Boxing Day 1993, LRT decided to operate the previous year's hybrid route from Queen Mary's Hospital via route R11 to Orpington, thence via route 208 to Bromley North. Because route number 211 became used for a new Waterloo – Hammersmith route earlier in the year, this Boxing Day special route carried number "201", and again was awarded to Metrobus. However, Roundabout was not deprived of work on Monday 26th December: a special contract was awarded to Roundabout to provide a service on far-flung route 272 (Woolwich – Thamesmead circular). Two Darts, DT32 & DT34 had the honour of fulfilling this unusual duty.

1994

Last Roundup Before Privatisation

RH5, RH7 and RH22 became useful spares and received rear blind boxes as part of a DipTac requirement to improve the bus environment throughout the capital.

Much attention was lavished on RH1 "Kestrel" during early 1994, in preparation for the Brighton Rally on 24th April. It was decided to apply a meticulous repaint one further time in maroon and grey with original Roundabout markings. Curiously, there was only one other London bus displayed at Brighton in 1994, and that was a further Selkent vehicle, LV12, a brand new Dennis Lance named "Enterprise", driven to the event by Bryan Constable. Both vehicles won awards, and RH1 was ceremoniously garlanded with flowers over her bonnet. As the Traffic Commissioner handed over the trophy, he whispered to Bryan "Now get the rest of the Selkent fleet up to that standard!" This was the last occasion Selkent / Roundabout exhibited vehicles from their fleet before privatisation; it was perhaps Bryan's last happy memory of Roundabout, in view of events later to unfold in 1994.

WMT no.632 continued to regularly perform on the R8 in February covering for FM3. No sooner had this Metrorider returned home, than FM8 had to be dispatched to Marshalls following collision on 26th March with a Metrobus Olympian on route 61 at the junction of Bromley Common with Turpington Lane!

David Hulls, winner of the 1993 "Midibus Driver of Year" award (working on route CE1 as the "Clatterford Clatterbus"), drove BL85 to the Blake Hall Spring Fair. However, by spring 1994 the MC refurbishment program was almost complete with MC1-4 having been treated, and the FMs returned from extensive repair. Consequently, on 20th May, BL85 performed her last duty with Roundabout, as OB28 working route R8 carrying a commemorative farewell headboard. The "old girl" had served her purpose very well, and returned next day to London United, operating the Hounslow garage Open Day specials. She then moved to Centrewest, and joined the last of her BL sisters in the training fleet at Westbourne Park (X).

The rear view (right) of RH7 "Swallow" in Station Square, Petts Wood, shows the blind box addition, and on close inspection, the "Mercedes Benz" name can be seen, but by no means was RH7 a Mercedes vehicle.

Due to difficulties in sourcing Robin Hood body spare parts, it was easier simply to cut an MC bumper down to size, and install Mercedes rear light clusters. FM5 "Taurus", just visible in shot, passes MC3, both on route R3. *Photo: Tom Gurney*

A visit to OB on Sunday 2nd October 1994 allows an opportunity to photograph RH1 for the first time under new ownership. The author wondered if this historic livery would be accepted or removed forthwith.
Photo: Tom Gurney

West Midlands loaned short Metrorider D632 NOE on route R8 in Orpington High Street. 20th January 1994.
Photo: K.Gurney

19th May 1994: the penultimate day of BL 85's stay with Roundabout shows a commemorative headboard fitted as she passes through St Mary Cray village on route R4. *Photo: G. Walker*

However, RH7 then expired and was sent to London Buses disposals at Fulwell, so the need arose for a replacement midibus. Former west London Reeves Burgess Mercedes mobility bus MT4 had been sent to Catford garage, to work the newly won mobility bus routes 931-7 / 970-973, whilst MW2/8/14 were converted to mobility bus specification. Having served her purpose at TL, Selkent earmarked MT4 as the replacement needed at OB, where Austin Blackburn organised careful removal of the rear wheelchair ramp and neatly masked-off the rear doors. Two 2-seater longitudinal seats were fitted in place of the wheelchair anchor points, and a cheery "welcome" sticker above the entrance door greeted passengers.

Significantly, MT4 had the distinction of being the final addition to the Roundabout fleet before privatisation. MT4 became the mainstay of route R8, and the combination of this unique vehicle with friendly regular driver, was a "must" for the young enthusiast to "do the Chelsfield loop"!

MT4 traverses Orpington High Street 3rd September 1994 – three days before privatisation. Unless any reader knows differently, this bus was route bound on the R8.
Photo: Tom Gurney

"Wash me ….. also available in red"

A visit to OB in 1994 to see 'Owl', and a last chance for a laugh under old ownership(!)
Photos: T. Gurney

Enter Stagecoach

During the latter part of 1994, London Buses sold off all its operating subsidiaries as part of the government's privatisation programme. However back in 1989, the Selkent Directors conducted extensive research, resulting in a fifty page report identifying the company's strengths, weaknesses, opportunities and threats, as a start to calculating a market value of the business. At this time, Selkent was already LBL's most efficient subsidiary in terms of mileage produced per pound of gross costs. It was no surprise that initial enquiries into the possibility of a management buy-out of Selkent from LBL were made. There was also known determination that Stagecoach Holdings PLC were particularly keen to acquire two of the capital's bus companies that were geographically close together. East London and Selkent were identified by the would-be purchaser and seen as ideal to make a suitable bid to be placed on them. As company Director of Selkent, Bryan made the personal decision not to be drawn into remortgaging his house for his stake in an auction against determined "big boys" and handed over the leadership of any Selkent internal bid to his trusted Finance Director, Mike Clayton. Mike worked hard at the project, but as soon as it was declared that Stagecoach was the preferred bidder, clearly the Selkent management bid application could never come into fruition. Stagecoach's 'wish list' of acquiring two London businesses became reality with the combined fleet of East London's and Selkent's 1,009 buses.

On 6th September 1994, the assets of Selkent, including its 406 strong fleet of buses, passed to the control of Stagecoach Holdings PLC. Included in the sale were the 32 Roundabout buses, comprising 13DT, 10FM, 5MC, 3RH and 1MT, and continuation of the lease on their Nugent Industrial Estate home. However, Stagecoach instantly dissolved Selkent Travel, thus eliminating the opportunity for drivers to demonstrate professional pride in their work. In concluding the private and chartered arm of the business, to which Roundabout had contributed, Plumstead's two RMCs, three coach seated Olympians, three coach seated ex-West Midlands Titans and numerous coaches were no longer required. Another instant change involved the installation of Stagecoach's own management personnel. After forty years with LT, Selkent's Managing Director Bryan Constable said "goodbye" to Roundabout and departed the Selkent scene.

November 1994 finds the Roundabout fleet under the banner of Stagecoach Selkent. MT4 is parked outside OB in the company of DT34 and MC1. Horton Tower in the St Mary Cray municipal estate overlooks the scene. *Photo: K. Gurney*

The first major change in appearance came on the 1st October 1994, when Bromley garage's Leyland Titan, T1034, freshly painted in an all red livery, appeared in Bromley to publicise the Christmas "Bromley Park & Ride" route B99. Plain unrelieved red with "Stagecoach Selkent" logos became the new livery for the company.

The first of the Roundabout fleet to be repainted into Stagecoach Selkent corporate livery were DT30 and DT32 respectively, happily retaining the 'ROUNDABOUT' fleet names on their sides. Soon following suit were DT28/31/40/55, and by August 1995, all of the fleet was repainted. The FM and MC classes however retained their white cantrail bands, having just the grey skirts painted over in red. RH1 victoriously retained maroon and grey livery.

White on red running number plates were introduced and accompanied the all red livery, but these seemed confined to OB, although black on yellow plates continued to show up at times.

The general opinion of staff was rather split. Some felt being part of a big group with powerful resources would bring bigger and better things; others felt privatisation as a whole was a bad thing for public transport. Rather cheekily, the fleetname on one TB vehicle had been altered to read "SOLDKENT"! In the main, drivers just got on with their jobs, but it was possible to detect some animosity over the change in style with which their business was being conducted, and an occasional bitter, less friendly air prevailed.

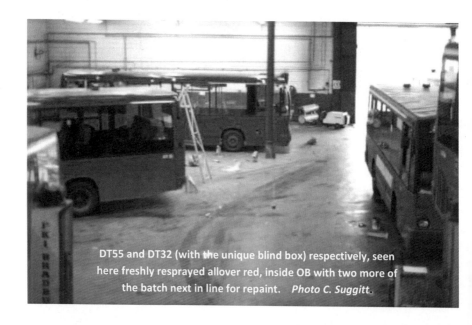

DT55 and DT32 (with the unique blind box) respectively, seen here freshly resprayed allover red, inside OB with two more of the batch next in line for repaint. *Photo C. Suggitt.*

Christmas Day 1994 finds RH1, 5 & 22 "the last of the originals" on the OB forecourt in the company of MT4 and MC1 & 5. *Photo: Tom Gurney*

Festive Season 1994

Having secured the contract to operate Bromley's seasonal "Park & Ride" service (dubbed route B99), Stagecoach Selkent made OB responsible for this Norman Park – Bromley High Street service.

From 1st October, this part-Bromley funded service ran on Saturdays only, becoming daily from 31st October. FM3, shown at the Bromley town terminus 1st October, was one of four initially deployed. *Photo: Tom Gurney*

Later in the season, RH vehicles were drafted in from Stagecoach United Counties, RH59, shown opposite, being the first of four from Kettering. *Photo: Chris Suggitt*

Boxing Day

For Boxing Day, Tuesday 26th December, LRT appeared tired of its hybrid route attempts. Route R11 was reinstated and operated by Roundabout, although between Queen Marys Hospital and Orpington Hospital only.

For the fourth year running, no service was provided on route 51, but Stagecoach Selkent operated route 208 over its full length Orpington – Lewisham. Metrobus ran its route 358 on a commercial basis.

1995: The Final 12 Months

1995 began with Nugent Estate Unit 5 resembling a spray paint booth as Roundabout's fleet took on Stagecoach Selkent's desired image, although large "*ROUNDABOUT*" logos continued to be applied to bus sides. Conversely, pending withdrawal, RH5 and 22 had their fleetnames removed. DT28 "Pride of Carlyle" lost her name as a result of the race to all-over red. The MC and FM types had their grey skirts painted out. RH 58-61 returned to Kettering after being laid-up for a month in OB, and MT4 said farewell to route R8 in March to begin a new career at TL on route 273. MC1 and MC2 were lent to TB for routes 314 & 336.

There was some concern at Roundabout, in view of the fact that the Orpington network was due for re-tender, including all routes operated by OB. How would their new masters, fresh to the London scene, respond to the invitation to bid? The expertise of Bryan Constable was no longer available (at least to Selkent – more of that later!). Interestingly, Roundabout decided not to conform to LRT's new requirement for "dayglow yellow" detail on all bus blinds, in view of this uncertainty. Metrobus, on the other hand, confidently converted all their fleet with the expectation (rightly so!) of retaining route 61.

The fresh specifications envisaged splitting routes R1 and R11 to operate independently at all times: R1 as Bromley Common to Grovelands, and R11 as Green Street Green to Queen Marys Hospital via Orpington Hospital and Tescos, thus introducing an evening and Sunday service to Grovelands. A Sunday service would also be provided on routes R3 and R4, with the Saturday late night single R3 projection beyond Green Street Green withdrawn. There were no changes proposed for routes R2 & R8, while routes R5 & R6 were excluded from this tendering round, having been awarded to Kentish Bus two years earlier. Although Kentish Bus had won route R7 as recently as November 1992, this route was included, for its structure and operation had not been successful. After six months, route 477 had been reintroduced between Orpington and Dartford. Route R7 was confined to run between Petts Wood and the St Mary Cray estates, yet performance over this residual section was giving concern. The resultant downturn in patronage led to the specification for route R7 being reduced from three to two buses per hour. Two big bus routes, 51 and 61, were also part of this tender tranche.

In late May, LRT delivered a knockout blow. No contracts were to be placed with Stagecoach Selkent. The Roundabout operation would surely be wound up. The midibus routes were awarded to Centrewest, Crystals and LondonLinks:

ROUTES R1, R3, R4 and R11 to CENTREWEST "Orpington Buses";

ROUTES R2 & R7 to CRYSTALS;

ROUTE R8 to LONDONLINKS.

ROUTE 61 was also awarded to Centrewest, a bodyblow to Metrobus which had performed outstandingly on this route since 1986.

ROUTE 51 was retained by London Central, which had operated the route since September 1992.

Stunned by the news, and with some uncertainty whether it was official or not, Roundabout staff were reduced to a state of high anxiety over their future. There was an early drive-in one evening, with buses coming off the road around 2000 while staff met to discuss the issues. Although this occurrence was not officially reported, it became common knowledge, and local passengers heard the following day, most with some kind of sympathy for the drivers.

It was a very sad time indeed, but eventually, reassurances were offered, with most Roundabout staff transferring to Centrewest along with the routes. Centrewest was made well aware of the driving team ethos responsible for the success of Roundabout. In a bid to perpetuate the enthusiasm of drivers agreeing to transfer, two main rotas were offered. One was a "common" rota, requiring staff to work across all the newly won routes covering all shifts including Sundays. Alternatively, drivers could elect to join the second rota, whereby staff would work only the "R" routes and were excluded from Sunday working. This second rota was a compromise attempt at maintaining Roundabout conditions of service, but stopping short of opportunities to become route-bound. Drivers agreeing to transfer were given type training and route learning opportunities in respect of route 61, whilst their places at Roundabout were covered by newly recruited Centrewest staff. However, a couple of drivers stayed on with Stagecoach Selkent moving to Bromley garage, and one 'old boy' driver resurfaced years later at Crystals as a regular on the R2.

By June, a Centrewest midibus (MA58) was seen in Orpington going over the routes on a route evaluation with company officials on board, the first tangible sign that changes were on the way. By the autumn, Crystals staff began route learning, and their brand new turquoise Mercedes vehicles could be frequently seen at locations such as Petts Wood.

Here, N601 JGP and N605 JGP wait at the Station Square stand opposite a somewhat "troubled" companion Mercedes cousin, MC5, on route R3. *Photo: K. Gurney*

The Roundabout fleet began to lose character and appeal. Small detail like the fleet numbers and pet names disappeared, most probably when buses were hand washed, causing these little inscriptions to peel away.

FM3 typifies the situation, having lost her name "Pisces" and most of her fleet number, seen on 18th November 1995 at the Nugent Estate.
Photo: A. Jeffreys

DT 39, seen at the Queen Marys Hospital stand, in early November, has been stripped of all decals in readiness for transfer to Catford Garage. *Photo: A. Jeffreys*

By August MC1 and MC4 lost their cherished WLT number plates during this time of great despondency.

Two of the remaining three RHs were withdrawn, and put into store at Bromley. At the beginning of November, DT39 moved to Catford garage as an additional spare for route P4. By mid November, four DTs moved to Bromley garage for route B99, for it was felt that the Park & Ride route would be best operated from there, as it was confirmed that OB would be closed down during the B99 contract. In their place, four Metroriders came to OB. Two were Optare bodied from Newcastle in Busways' yellow and white livery. The other two were MR27 and MR46, ousted from Catford Garage by the arrival of ex-OB's MT4 and DT39; interestingly, these shorter MCW bodied Metroriders had already been repainted by the TL coachmaker's shop into Stagecoach's provincial white livery with orange, blue and red stripes, and modified with a larger blind box, again intended for Busways. It is notable to record that Stagecoach "white 'n' stripes" finally bestowed itself on Roundabout, if only for the last few weeks' service.

Above: The two Newcastle Busways MRLs on routes R1 and R11 caught together on 18th November 1995, amongst the 1950s housing along Chipperfield Road, typical of St Pauls Cray estate. *Below:* Former LBL MR46, seen on route R1 in Orpington High Street on the last day of Roundabout, had received a full Stagecoach provincial livery, in readiness for a new life outside London. *Photos: A. Jeffreys*

Saturday 2nd December was to be the start date for the new contracts. On Friday 1st December, the last day of Roundabout, RH1 'Kestrel', with a commemorative headboard affixed to her radiator grill, duly performed as OB1 on route R1 throughout the morning. A defective interior light fitting required "Kestrel" to be subbed during the day.

After taking a rest back at OB during the afternoon while the defect was rectified, a special honour was bestowed on "Kestrel": she was chosen to be the last ever Roundabout bus in service. Accordingly, she was allocated the evening R1 duty which after finishing at Bromley Common, proceeded light to Petts Wood Station Square to perform the 0037 R3 to Cray Avenue: the last scheduled duty of the day to return to OB. "Kestrel" entered her home for the last time at 00.45 in the early hours of Saturday, 2nd December.

Above: RH1 with a few late night passengers, ready to depart the final Roundabout journey, over route R3 at 00:37, 2nd December 1995. *Photo: K.Gurney*

Below: DT 30, the last Dart to return to base, in the process of being deblinded. *As Austin holds the vehicle withdrawal tick sheet, Andy smiles for the camera. Photo: A. Jeffreys*

The FMs were collected the following evening for a new life elsewhere within the mighty Stagecoach group, and that left just one vehicle, RH1, to be driven to Catford garage, withdrawn from service, and put up for sale. This done, Austin Blackburn and his workshop colleague Andy Ewing were given a week to complete their final responsibility of asset stripping Unit 5 of its bus garage status, in order to return it to original condition (as an empty warehouse), typically a provision of a lease agreement. With all buses dispersed, the many 'component bins' were slid out of their neat shelf dividers and sent to supplement the spares inventories at Plumstead and Catford. Finally, a decision had to be made regarding OB's two inspection lifts. One was sent to Plumstead, and the other (much older) shipped out for Stagecoach Kenya Bus at their Eastleigh depot!

The small timber office home of the engineering team was demolished in spectacular fashion. Andy took the controls of their fork lift truck and positioned the forks level with the windows. At that point, Roy Sewell chose to telephone, answered by Austin just as Andy raised the forks. As the structure toppled, Austin decided to make a hasty exit! That, they say, was OB's last communication....

The New Operators:

Centrewest London Buses Limited was the result of a successful management buyout led by Peter Hendy during privatisation of London Buses in 1994. The company felt that it had by no means to confine activities to its "traditional" west London operating area, and decided to bid for the Orpington network, armed with the statistics which created Roundabout whilst Peter was a member of Bryan Constable's team back in 1985. With a further ironic twist, the brand "Orpington Buses" was to be adopted for Centrewest's new venture, the very same name from which Roundabout's garage code "OB" was derived.

Centrewest did not find it easy to establish a base in the Orpington area. Planning application for an operating centre on waste land at Crittall's Corner was refused. Consideration was given to using the former Jasons Coaches "shed" next door to Metrobus at Green Street Green, however, with deadlines approaching, the former LCBS Swanley (SJ) garage was hastily resurrected, having stood semi-derelict for many years pending planning decisions.

In the meantime, the former Ebdons Coaches yard at Foots Cray was utilised as a training base, with an M-type MCW Metro, a new Dennis Dart (DP), and a Mercedes midibus (MA), allocated for route and type training purposes.

Both Photos: A. Jeffreys

Centrewest clearly made a bold move to demonstrate their company profile in the new operating area, with RML885 and RML2735 working route 61 on the first day, with the former even making an appearance into Petts Wood on midibus route R3! Who ever said it couldn't be done?

Centrewest operations therefore commenced on 2nd December using a rather distant garage, although a paying-in room was established above the Bookmaker's emporium beside St Mary Cray station! This situation prevailed for several months before permission was secured to relocate to a permanent site at Faraday Way, coded "Y", a stone's throw from the former OB premises the other side of Cray Avenue!

Crystals of Dartford was keen to make a comeback to stage bus work in the area, having given up route 858 in 1986 to Roundabout as route R2, and losing route 146 (Bromley – Downe) to Metrobus in 1991. Once considered a possible contender for the original 1986 tender round due to their strong position with a base at Bridge Road in the heart of the Orpington network, the company had since moved to larger premises some distance away at 127 Dartford Road.

Crystals had a strong association with mobility bus and special needs work, and therefore were seen as an empathic transport provider, deserved of a reminder from LRT about the bids being invited for work in Orpington.

Despite congratulating themselves on effectively winning back their Biggin Hill – Orpington route, and gaining route R7, there were some self-recriminations at Crystals over their bid for route R8. Crystals had mistakenly costed the R8 as a two-bus operation, yet the route only required single vehicle operation! Bernie Costello was "headhunted" as Operations Manager for the newly won R2/R7. However, before his arrival, the decision had been made to order brand new Mercedes vehicles with *manual* transmission. As a result, recruitment of bus drivers was not easy! Consequently, Bernie worked many shifts behind the wheel, often unpaid, believing anyway that the routes can be better run by doing the work yourself!

LondonLinks Buses Ltd had only been established in January, mostly comprising the Kentish Bus and London & Country operations on LRT tendered work from Walworth, Croydon and Dunton Green Garages. The company was a subsidiary of Kentish Bus, which was experiencing some embarrassment over their ailing Lewisham (LM) operations. Never-the-less, their new subsidiary was given the opportunity to operate route R8, using Metroriders from LondonLinks' Dunton Green garage.

Metrobus

Metrobus was keen to take on all the tendered "R" routes, using Optare Metroriders and Darts. During research for this book, it transpired that Metrobus engaged a consultant for the task of formulating bids for the midibus routes on offer. No longer associated with Selkent, the inspiration behind the original "Rising Star" / "Roundabout" operation, Bryan Constable, deployed his infinite knowledge of Orpington's midibus network in an effort to secure the contracts for Metrobus. Despite this unbeatable expertise, success in this round of tendering eluded Metrobus, furthermore, LRT appeared to snub the impeccable service record by awarding route 61 to Centrewest. Metrobus' performance on route 61 had been immaculate since operations commenced the day Roundabout was born, 16th August 1986.

Gary Wood, joint Managing Director of Metrobus, was said to have telephoned his joint counterpart Peter Larking on holiday to break the news. Gary simply said "We haven't won anything, Peter". "I don't believe you," was Peter's response, "We've surely retained the 61? You *are* joking?"

For nine years, Metrobus and Roundabout had created the highest reputation for LRT's operations in the Orpington area; clearly, advice to take into account proven good performance had been disregarded.

Unsurprisingly, the enterprising gentlemen at Metrobus refused to concede defeat. A route 610 (nomenclature from the year 1933!) was announced, running between Chislehurst and Bromley, in direct competition with route 61. The only legal criteria Metrobus had to satisfy was to register such a route as a commercial operation. Metrobus was convinced its reputation would encourage clientelle to remain loyal to blue and yellow buses on route 61, despite the fact that cash fares only would be accepted.

As noted, Centrewest was experiencing difficulty finding suitable premises in the Orpington area. With yet more irony, the former Jasons Coaches premises were part of the Metrobus fold – little wonder there was no inclination to accept Centrewest as tenants! A further emphatic "No" was delivered to LRT following a red-faced request to continue operating route 61 for a further six months owing to Centrewest's predicament. However, towards the end of 1995, Kentish Bus surrendered many contracts operated by its consistently under-performing Lewisham base. Possibly in a bid to sweeten Metrobus, Kentish Bus midibus routes 138, 181, 284, and most significantly, double deck route 161, were offered to Metrobus. The offer was duly accepted at the Kentish Bus tender rates, and with work secured for Metrobus' Olympian fleet, nothing further was heard of route 610.

However, at the 1996 annual Cobham Museum bus rally, Metrobus cheekily exhibited a Dart displaying "610 Chislehurst" in its blind box!

Photo: K. Gurney

History of the Robin Hoods (RH)

Vehicle specifications:

Chassis: Iveco Daily 49-10

Engine: Iveco 2.45 litre

Bodywork: Robin Hood 21 seats

(RH1/23/24 coach seated)

The great deal Bryan Constable secured with Robin Hood envisaged the purchase of twenty-four Iveco RHs to meet Roundabout's requirements. However, the Optare City Pacer had caught the imagination of LRT, which specified five examples of this type to be ordered for routes R3 and R6. Although Roundabout's RH complement was therefore reduced to twenty, Robin Hood Vehicle Builders Ltd, the Southampton based marine company, went ahead with the manufacture of all twenty-four in this initial batch, all of which were accepted by LRT.

The fast pace of the production of these new buses ensured that RH1 (upholstered in Holdsworth's "classic quality" moquette) was ready by mid April, just in time to be exhibited at the annual Brighton coach show. The vehicle was the first to show-off Roundabout's maroon and grey livery with "*ROUNDABOUT*" fleetnames, and sported the pet name "Kestrel", just as Bryan had promised his son to take up the practice of naming the individual vehicles making up the Roundabout fleet. "Kestrel" spent the next four months as the flagship model for LRT publicity, and evaluation of the new Orpington midibus routes.

Left: At the Robin Hood Racing workshop, Southampton, an RH body is assembled upon an Iveco chassis. *Photo: Brian Champion of Robin Hood Racing.*

Above: Before leaving the factory, an error in blind production was spotted: the destination should read "Knockholt Pound"!

Right: With no clues to her identity, a completed RH waits in the sun outside her birthplace. *Photos: Austin Blackburn*

RH2-7, 18 and 21 commenced the order for vehicles with conventional bus seats in "Firths Colour pattern no. 5607" moquette, coming off the production line at the Iveco factory in Winsford, Cheshire by mid June, and driven direct to Nugent Industrial Estate Unit 17, the "home of Roundabout". The remaining RHs, upon completion at the end of June, were sent into temporary storage at Aldenham Works, to avoid swamping the emerging operating centre at Unit 17, which was still in the process of being fitted out with office and workshop facilities.

Upon arrival at OB, a late discovery of a roof defect required some swift action with a rivet gun before the RH fleet was deemed ready for service. But with everything in place for the inaugural day, Saturday 16th August 1986 saw the Robin Hoods on the road fully operational.

However, the four surplus Robin Hoods, RH 14/19/20/22 in green and grey primer, were held back at Aldenham, in anticipation for possible projects elsewhere. These vehicles enjoyed the dubious distinction of being amongst the last residents at Aldenham, as in November, the "great LT cathedral" on 55 acres, closed its doors after thirty years' distinguished service. In the post-privatisation era, there was no perceived need for a centralised overhaul and storage facility.

With no immediate future envisaged with London Buses, the four spare RHs were leased to Eastbourne Buses for their "Red Carpet" service. They were appropriately decked out internally with red carpeting, and treated externally to Eastbourne Buses' "aircraft blue and biscuit" livery, a colour scheme which two years later would play a major part in bus tendering elsewhere. Such was the success of "Red Carpet" that the 21 seat Robin Hoods were replaced by larger buses. After just three months, RHs 14, 19 and 22 were returned off-lease, and sent to Selkent District headquarters at Camberwell, while RH20 remained with Eastbourne at little longer. RHs 14 and 19 were repainted into Roundabout livery.

RH14 was duly named "Nightingale" and joined the fleet at OB. However, RH19 was promptly repainted yet again into a blue livery to meet a last minute change of plan. RH22 was also treated to the blue livery, and the pair sent initially to Battersea (B) garage for the "Chelsea Harbour" route C3, which commenced in April 1987, later transferring to the basement (VB) of Gillingham Street (GM) garage.

Eleven Roundabout Robin Hoods, RH11-18,21,23,24, were earmarked for transfer to Bexleybus, and took up bonnet numbers in the range 65-76 in the BB fleet. In November 1987, the task of repainting into "aircraft blue and biscuit" livery was undertaken by Eastbourne Buses, which conveniently had the necessary tins of paint in ample stock! RH17 "Snipe" was the first RH to leave OB, and was deployed as a driver training bus at Bexleyheath (BX) garage. The new element of the Bexleybus midi fleet was a batch of short Metroriders delivered in advance of BB's January 1988 start date. These MRs were sent to OB for routes R1/R11 to cover for the departing RHs until their replacement MRLs arrived. Blue and biscuit thus appeared briefly in Orpington!

104

RH17 "Snipe", parked up just short of its actual terminus, seen here by the Petrol station in Green Street Green, not long before the bus was moved out to Bexleybus. Note 37p for a litre of petrol! *Photo: E.L. Collinson*

In early 1988, the RH fleet at Roundabout received a fresh coat of maroon and grey paint but sadly lost the distinctive white lining. Furthermore, they appeared without fleetnames and numbers for some time, until eventually gaining more simple, cheaper logos, in "Crillie" typeface, applied to the sides. RH10 "Wren" was sent to BX for training and eventually became a permanent member of the Bexleybus fleet as no.64.

RH10 "Wren", with the white piping, on route R2. The "London Regional Transport Service" sticker, with familiar roundel, was applied to reassure passengers that whatever livery worn by an approaching bus, it was part of the unified network! *Photo: K.Gurney*

Above: The rear of RH7 "Swallow" demonstrating the neat company signwriting adorning the Robin Hood body, complemented by the helpful addition of a route number board. 14th November 1987.

Below: Around midday on 18th May 1989, there was just enough room for RH 8 "Swan" (with signwriting in new Crillie font) to nest in behind Plumstead's resident Olympian L128 on route 161, and Boroline's ex-Ipswich Atlantean no.84 "Agincourt" performing Tesco's free bus service T1 to Crittalls Corner, Foots Cray. Compare the diagonal line of the rear "Roundabout" strap between the two years! *Photos: K. Gurney*

On paper, all 24 RHs had been allocated 'pet names' of birds. However, towards the end of 1989, three names remained to be applied: "Canary" (RH19), "Teal" (RH20), and "Jay" (RH22). However, their intended names were *not* applied; instead, names from Robin Hoods sent to Bexleybus were reused. When entering service at OB in January 1990, RH19 had been christened "Sandpiper" (carried by RH18) and RH22 "Hawk" (carried by RH23). In 1994, RH22 was named for third time: she emerged from a fresh coat of red paint carrying RH9's former name "Heron"!

"Teal" remained unaccounted for, owing to the fact that its intended recipient, RH20 never carried its bonnet number, nor even turned a wheel for Roundabout, staying instead at Eastbourne after departure from Aldenham. RH20 earned a bizarre reputation as the "Secret Bexleybus", for its part in an exercise, which for commercial and industrial reasons, had to remain confidential at the time. Selkent's response to LRT's invitation to bid for the Bexleyheath / Woolwich tenders in 1987 was to draw up a prospectus detailing the Bexleybus proposal.

To illustrate the mix of new and acquired vehicles for the new operation, the prospectus contained a photograph of a line-up of a selection of such buses from the Eastbourne fleet, whose livery would be closely adopted for Bexleybus.

Thus RH20 had "*Bexleybus*" logos affixed to her sides as she was paraded in secrecy for the photographic session at Eastbourne with her companions. After a "wardrobe malfunction", word got out, and a mystical air surrounded RH20 throughout her eventual career with Bexleybus!

A Bexleybus liveried RH appeared briefly in service at OB, in the shape of RH21 serving on route R3 in June 1989, simply displaying "3" in the blind box.

RH1-9 were painted into red LBL livery with white band and grey skirt, during the winter of 1989 into Spring 1990. When the Bexleybus operation ceased in 1991, RH15, already in red livery, was reunited with her sisters at Roundabout and correctly regained its original name "Kingfisher". Whilst at BX, RH15 had been fitted with a new engine and substantial front end repairs (leaving her devoid of "Iveco" badges) following a road traffic accident.

RH15 back in Roundabout livery, bearing its original name "Kingfisher", on a clockwise R5 loop, pausing at the Bull's Head, Pratts Bottom, 20th April 1993. Rushmore Hill was once the turnpike from London to Hastings, and a toll house was located just behind RH15.
Photo: K. Gurney

During its final days with Roundabout, RH4 had the honour of being the last of its class to be painted into red. In May 1992, RH1 "Kestrel" was treated to a full refurbishment including a change of seat moquette carried out at Hants & Dorset Trim, from orange/red fabric to purple/grey stripe colour. RH1 became something of a record breaker, receiving five repaints in her nine years' service with Roundabout (a fresh coat of maroon & grey in 1988, red repaints in 1990 and 1991, an attempt to recreate original maroon & grey appearance on refurbishment a year later, and finally Showbus standard maroon & grey in 1994).

On delivery in 1993, the ten FMs were intended to replace the remaining RHs at Roundabout (RH1-9/15/19/22). These RHs even carried "for sale" notices inside the buses for passengers to read! Most were sold to Luton & District. RH8 did not get far after overheating and catching fire in the Dartford Tunnel, and was scrapped as a result. However as RH5 and RH7 had extensive rebuilds prior to the FM arrivals, including new floors and chassis repairs, the decision was made to retain them at OB with RH1 and RH22. As body spares were now becoming scarce, Mercedes parts were cut to size and fitted. Notably, RH7 and RH22 sported Mercedes Benz rear bumpers and badges! By May 1994, RH7 was withdrawn and sent to the the Fulwell disposals department, leaving three into the final year. RH7 was the last bus to leave OB before privatisation.

With just three RHs left as spares at OB, it was not surprising that they were becoming less used, for drivers were becoming spoiled by the FM's power assisted steering, a feature not incorporated in the RH class. However, a modification had been made to RH22s front suspension to make manual steering lighter, with the result that the bus appeared elevated at the front end! A minor source of amusement appreciated by Bob Muir on his visits to OB was the sight of a plastic cash bag secured by means of an elastic band over the gear lever knob; a practice -"tradition" even –enabling drivers to overcome the unpleasant sticky feel of the RH gearstick grip.

In October 1994, the RH fleet at OB was boosted by the allocation of four Robin Hoods from United Counties for the purpose of operating the Bromley "Park & Ride" seasonal service B99 until January 1995. These were 23 seat vehicles, sprayed into red, and on paper allocated numbers RH58/59/60/61.

With the FMs working well on the R2/R4/R8 with occasional use on the other routes, RH5 and RH22 became rarely used. They were withdrawn in the Spring of 1995 and laid up at Bromley garage, thus leaving just one Robin Hood, RH1 "Kestrel". On inspection of RH1's last engineering service log of 11th November 1995, she had clocked up 358,977 km during her 9 years service. Having served at Roundabout continuously since the first day, it was rightfully her privilege to carry a commemorative headboard inscribed "Last Day of Roundabout" and to perform the very last Roundabout journey of all, the 0037 R3 service from Petts Wood to Cray Avenue. She survives at the time of writing; her subsequent history is reported in the chapter "The Survivors."

Dubbed RH58 whilst on loan for the 1994 Bromley Park & Ride seasonal service, this former United Counties (no. 58) Robin Hood differed from its Roundabout counterparts in not having an off-side cab door. In plain Stagecoach red, RH58 waits for passengers at Elmfield Road town terminus.
Photo: Tom Gurney

The RH was a versatile vehicle that turned up on all routes. The manual transmission was clearly more robust than the original OV stablemate, and the hardy build of the Iveco chassis meant many RH entered service with other UK operators after withdrawal from London. The OB engineering team was sorry to see them drift away, and Bryan Constable stated that the RH was the first operational small bus capable of covering the driver's wages!

Front end comparison of Roundabout's first and last Iveco midibus types, as RH5&22 pose outside OB with FM10 in November 1994.
Photo: Tom Gurney

By strange coincidence 'The Robin Hoods of Orpington' was an appropriate theme identifying with the area of housing east of Poverest Road traversed by route R3. There were many satisfied and grateful patrons from Robin Hood Green, Forest Way, Friar Rd, Lockesley Drive, Little John Rd, Archer Road, Marion Crescent and Hood Avenue! The author suggests that sometime in the future, little buses with names such as "Maid Marion" or "Little John" will go round and round the area.....

History of the Optare City Pacers (OV)

Chassis: Volkswagen LT55

Engine: Volkswagen 2.4 litre

Bodywork: Optare City Pacer 25 seats

Optare was established in February 1985, as the result of the purchase from Leyland of the former Charles H. Roe coachbuilding facility at Crossgates in Leeds. The new company specialised in purpose-built midibus construction, and was keen to steer away from the beleaguered "breadvan" midibus image. This progressive company enlisted the help of Leeds College of Art students, who created this very stylish look to Optare's first product. The City Pacer LT55 won Optare the 'Bus of the Year' accolade, together with its coach version counterpart, the Inter-City Pacer.

Deregulation brought considerable change to the bus industry, and Optare felt their new bus satisfied a market niche for a small bus offering large bus standards, but with lower operating costs. Many City Pacers were snapped up by new 'opportunist' operators and older established companies alike throughout the provinces. Optare succeeded in impressing LRT, which decided to order five of these manual gearbox 25-seaters for new route R3, including one spare, which would be utilised on route R6.

A City Pacer under construction at Optare's Leeds plant in June 1990, nearing the end of the LT55 production run.

Photo: K. Gurney

The type code "OV" (Optare Volkswagen) was devised, and in July 1986, OV1 and OV2 in Roundabout maroon and grey livery (with standard bus *bench* seats) were duly delivered from the Volkswagen plant at Swindon to Selkent headquarters at one, Warner Road, Camberwell for publicity purposes, carrying large "OPTARE" logo boards in the saloon windows. OV3/4/5 (with coach-style *squab* seating) soon followed suit and were put into store at Aldenham, although OV5 was not registered until August, so the C555LMW index reserved for OV5 was not used and a "D" registration plate was assigned. Bryan's son had chosen the names of windstorms for the OV class, and these were applied before the vehicles were sent to OB. After fifteen months' operation, it is curious to note that another hurricane swept the streets of Orpington as the most destructive windstorm for decades passed across southern England one night in October 1987! A principle in practice here, as the budding young bus enthusiast, curious over the name on the side of OV2, learned about the destructive powers of a *real* hurricane from the flying slates and falling trees all around him!

Once in service at Roundabout, these vehicles exhibited some serious shortcomings. Surprisingly the chassis was rather less robust than the Iveco. Much smaller brake pads featured too. Its six cylinder engine demonstrated peculiarly poor low-speed torque, requiring more gear changing, using a dubious cable operated gear change necessitated by the rebuilt driving position. Engine inaccessibility earned the disfavour of engineers, as did the need for frequent clutch renewals because drivers avoided too many gear changes.

Hill starts encountered on route R3 in Poverest Road and at Chelsfield Station required considerable dexterity on the part of drivers. The long handbrake lever on the right of the cab had to be released right down to floor level whilst finding the clutch "bite" point using high revs to overcome the insufficient torque; by walking pace, another gear had to be found – quickly – using the gear stick on the left side - to avoid coming to a standstill again. Only three-handed drivers could manage the steering wheel in addition! Drivers likened gear finding to "stirring a bowl of wallpaper paste", and the stresses imposed on the long gear stick resulted in a case of one shearing-off near floor level: Ernie Bunclarke was seen leaning from the cab window of his immobilised City Pacer waving his trophy at bemused passengers on a passing R3!

By early 1990, most vehicles had succumbed to corporate LBL red, but OV5 "Whirlwind" continued to exhibit all the traditional "Roundabout" features as seen here: full maroon and grey livery and seat moquette; the special font devised in house for the "Roundabout" decals; and its name in "Palace Script". The driver is wearing his company maroon anorak, and beside him rests his Selkent holdall. The crisp 1990 winter morning finds plenty of passengers for this R3 journey (with "new fares in operation") as it arrives at Orpington Pond, source of the River Cray. *Photo: K. Gurney*

Patience in the workshop at Unit 17 and on the road was wearing somewhat thin. In late 1989, an opportunity arose to replace the five original manual OVs with automatic transmission versions. Four such OVs became spare when London Country North East surrendered LRT tendered Camden Hoppa route C2. These had been delivered new in plain red livery with MBV ("Minibus Volkswagen" – LCBS nomenclature) fleet numbers in March 1987 to LCNW's outstation at the Homespeed Yard, Muswell Hill. They entered service in this condition at OB, but in January 1990, they were treated to a new coast of red paint with grey skirt, white lining and yellow doors, and fleet numbers OV26, 38, 44 and 49 applied.

OV1-4 were repainted into red livery, and OV1, highly prone to breaking down, was quickly pensioned off to the training fleet at Plumstead (PD) garage, followed by OV2 & OV3 in November / December 1989 and OV4 in January 1990. OV5 soldiered on in service at OB for a few months longer, and at this stage, became the last original Roundabout vehicle still in maroon and grey; however, this distinction was lost when RH1 was returned to original livery a couple of years later. However, the automatic transmission OVs failed to live up to expectations. They lacked power, and seemed tired from their service on route C2. A decision was taken to reinstate a couple of original manual City Pacers. OV5 which had been mothballed at OB, succumbed to a red repaint, and returned to service in March 1990. OV2 left PD in April 1990 and also returned to OB for further service. Therefore two original manual OVs ran in red livery, minus their names, during the spring, before being allocated in June to the training fleet at PD.

A clear need had emerged for a replacement type for route R3. Four Mercedes 811D with Carlyle bodies (MC class) were ordered, and a one-for-one swap occurred during September 1990, allowing cascade of OV38/44/49 to replace OV1-5 as PD trainers. OV26 was sent to Barking garage (BK) for training duties.

Bryan felt that an original Roundabout vehicle should be represented among the exhibits under the safe custody of the LT Museum. OV2 'Hurricane' was the lucky candidate for preservation, and was rightfully returned to the Roundabout team for a full sand-down, repaint into Roundabout maroon and grey livery, with an internal retrim. She was exhibited in July 1991 at the Plumstead garage Open Day, where official handover to the LT Museum took place. "Hurricane" was stored as part of the museum's reserve collection at Acton, and displayed at the March 2002 Open Day.

Whilst the Acton Depot was refurbished during 2008/9, OV2 was moved with other exhibits to the Science Museum's "large objects" site at the former RAF Broughton airfield. "Hurricane" moved back to Acton on completion of the work to rejoin her venerable companions.

However, OV3 'Tornado' was the preferred preservation choice from the engineer's point of view, as out of the five originals, this was in the best condition. But OV3 had a redesigned gear linkage, which perhaps was seen as not in keeping with the LT55 mechanical design, and therefore was not a true representative of the type.

After a little over a year's service with Plumstead's training school, the Roundabout OVs departed one by one. OV4 "Chinook", which had been a favourite with drivers and passengers, retired first in March 1991, and sadly ended her days at the Fire Research Establishment at Borehamwood. Two months later, OV1 "Typhoon" went to a similar fate at the Fire Research Establishment at Cardington, Bedfordshire. OV3 "Tornado" and OV5 "Whirlwind" saw further PSV service with other operators, although OV5 was withdrawn within months after fire damage in Scotland. OV3 still survives, privately owned as a caravan! It seems an unhappy conclusion for one of the original Roundabout types, admired for its stylish appearance, that three out of the five examples should fall victim to fire. Of the automatic examples, OV49 was purchased by "Little Jim's Buses of Berkhamsted", but proved forever troublesome in service, finally disgracing itself by expiring yards from its garage entrance after a day's duty! The owner was so exasperated that he left it where it was and told a pal with a tow truck next morning to "take it away and do what you please with it!"

OV4 "Chinook" on route R7 passes under the railway bridge at Tudor Way, Petts Wood on 13th September 1988. This bridge suffered two strikes by double deckers whilst in service on route 208: T682 (TL) in 1985, and T110 (TB) in 1993. *Photo: K. Gurney*

The Red Dodges (A)

Vehicle Specifications

Chassis: Dodge 50 S56C

Engine: Perkins 4.05 litre

Bodywork: Rootes of Maidstone 19 seats

Built: 1982

Five years on from the successful minibus trials in suburban London, a local route requiring an allocation of two midibuses was introduced in London Transport's northernmost outpost, Potters Bar in Hertfordshire. A pair of FS minibuses inaugurated route PB1 in March 1977, but typically became life expired after a few years. During the quest to replace them, Bryan Constable, whose remit at the time included responsibility for PB, was approached by Dodge sales specialists, eager to enter the midibus market. Bryan advised them to offer a model with a tough engine and a refined automatic transmission with a long life expectancy. Dodge was a listening organisation, and presented their 50 S56C with a good sized four litre engine and a Chrysler Torqueflite gearbox from USA applications. Two of these Dodge 19 seat vehicles were ordered, built at the Bedford Truck & Bus factory, Luton, arriving in January 1983. They were numbered A1 & A2 and given the registrations NYN1Y and NYN2Y respectively. Although remarkably competent technically, the pair remained unique, for by then, competitors had established themselves, and drivers did not aspire to the amount of bodywork to their right: the driving position was too close to the centre-line of the vehicle.

When no longer needed at Potters Bar as a result of LT losing Route PB1 to North Mimms Coaches, they came south to Catford. Here, prior to the opening of Nugent Park Unit 17, driver assessment, training and route learning for the Roundabout operation was based. They remained at Catford as operational spares in readiness to support OB's operations when needed.

A2 arrived at OB in November 1986 and served until February 1987, when it was returned to Catford garage (TL) for driver training and route learning on the impending Lewisham midibus network. However, it was immediately replaced at OB by A1, which only stayed a couple of months, before both A1 and A2 were despatched to the Gillingham Street Basement garage (VB – later becoming GB) to serve on central London midibus route C1. But by November 1987 there was greater need for their presence at Orpington, and the pair returned to OB where they worked together to back up the Roundabout fleet into 1988.

In May 1988, A1 again left OB for driver familiarisation purposes firstly at Harrow Weald (HW) garage, then at Bexleyheath, before reuniting with her sister back at Orpington in July. In August, they together left OB for the last time, moving back to the basement at Gillingham Street (GB) for use on route C1.

Their stint on route C1 lasted a few months before sent on loan to Greater Manchester for a few weeks. On return to London, they were mothballed for several years at Westbourne Park (X) garage.

These two vehicles humbly played an important part in the development of the small bus ideology in London. They not only saw active service on a range of routes from the outer suburbs to central London, filling in as operational spares whenever necessary, but supported all manner of training and route testing, clocking up a respectable mileage in doing so. Their somewhat utilitarian appearance failed to gain them the dignity they deserved, yet their "Jack of All Trades" role should be acknowledged. Internally, the seats were of LT block pattern moquette (Titan style) with a rather ostentatious leatherette edging feature. Any prospect of preservation seems unlikely, for both vehicles are now untraceable, after A1 passed to the former Head of Bus Disposal ("Arthur Daley") at Fulwell, and A2 was sold for educational purposes to Willesden Engineering College.

A1 sits at Station Square, Petts Wood, overlooked by the railway booking office, which was extended a year later. On route R3, 7th July 1988, there seems little doubt the A1 is deputising for a "mechanical" OV? *Photo: K. Gurney*

A2 passes Goodrich ironmongers, a long established Orpington High Street name, at the start of an anti-clockwise loop of route R5 (at the time of writing, this direction of working had been assigned route number R10). 9th December 1987 *Photo: K.Gurney*

History of the MCW Metrorider (MRL)

Vehicle Specifications

Chassis: MCW Metrorider

MF158/1 (65-73)

MF158/2 (74-76 coach seated)

MF158/14 (77)

Engine: Cummins 6B series 5.9 litre

Body: Metro Camell Weymann (MCW) 33 seats

Metro Camell Weyman (MCW) created a purpose built vehicle at the height of the midibus revolution, responding to a need for higher capacity vehicles throughout the UK. MCW utilised many common Ford components: the dashboard and steering wheel were identical to the Ford Cargo lorry, for example. Bus engineers always applaud accident prone items being sourced from the parts bins of a volume produced model, so OB was delighted to find the rear light clusters were from the brand new Ford Cabriolet Mk IV, and headlights from the relaunched Consul and Granada.

Twelve "stretched" 33 seat Metroriders (MRL) were ordered to relieve capacity difficulties on routes R1 / R11. However, Bexleybus' own 25 seat Metroriders were delivered in November / December 1987, and nine were temporarily allocated to OB to allow Robin Hoods RH 10-18/21/23/24 to leave the Roundabout fleet to be despatched to Eastbourne for repaint in readiness for transfer to Bexleybus. A new numbering sequence was devised for the Bexleybus fleet, 29-40 being carried by the new Metroriders, of which 29-37 served at OB as follows:

BB29/30 (E929/30KYR) & BB31/32/33 (E631/2/3KYW) Nov 1987–Jan 1988

BB34/35/36/37 (E634/5/6/7KYW) Dec 1987 – Jan 1988

BB29-40 later became MR53-64 when painted red years later at BX.

Bexleybus 32 was one of nine new Metroriders temporarily based at OB to free-up a number of Roundabout's RH, such as RH11 following, to go for repaint prior to transfer to Bexleybus. Orpington High Street, 31st December 1987.
Photo: K. Gurney

Roundabout's own MRLs were delivered from 16th January 1988, and put to work immediately on routes R1 / R11. At the same time, E76TDA, a 25 seater MCW Metrorider demonstrator vehicle was lent to assist bedding-in the new type of vehicle, also proving useful as a spare to support the failing OV class on route R3. Although delivered in full Roundabout finish, the MRLs were not given bonnet numbers immediately. A "local" fleet numbering scheme appeared, awarding three "M43", "M44", and "M97", but after repaint into red, they acquired numbers MRL 65-76. MRL77 joined OB in August 1988 as the sole 'F' plate Roundabout MRL from a batch of sixteen that were destined for Westlink.

The greater capacity on offer by these machines was greatly appreciated by the regular passengers in the St Pauls Cray estate. The MRL offered 33 wider seats compared with the RH's 21 seats, with more space for shopping and luggage and a greater circulation area. Three provided coach-style seating. All but two carried the bird names from the RHs they replaced, emulating the fine maritime tradition of adding the Roman suffix "II" by way of respect to the former carrier, for example "Kingfisher II". However the naming of the MRL fleet was somewhat inconsistent, for the name sequence of the RH class was not replicated on the MRLs, and duplicating of names such as "Seagull" occurred.

As well as appearances by Metroriders from outside London (demonstrators E76 TDA and G689 KNW, West Midlands 632, plus four examples to cover the last days of Roundabout), four 25 seat MRs in red livery from the LBL fleet, allocated as "float" vehicles for Selkent's use, also served as operational spares at OB:

MR14 (D474 PON) April 1992 – April 1993 (gaining *"ROUNDABOUT"* logos)

MR35 (E135 KYW) October 1993 – November 1993

MR38 (E138 KYW) November 1992 – January 1993

MR51 (E151 KYW) September 1993 – January 1994.

Just days old, E646 KYW (before its identity was revealed as MRL70 "Seagull") takes up an allocation on route R11, gingerly progressing into the War memorial stop as the driver familiarises himself with this new, longer vehicle type. 27th January 1988.
Photo: K. Gurney

MRL 65 (unamed) and 75 "Woodpecker II" were the first Roundabout MRLs to appear in Corporate red in April 1990, the resprays being carried out at unit 5, with the remainder being so treated by July.

Although the Metrorider provided much needed relief to the capacity problems on routes R1/R11, the heavy loads never-the-less generated a number of stress issues on the stretched Metrorider, particularly the rear suspension mountings. Furthermore, the hot summer of 1988 brought unforseen start-up problems (due to fuel vaporisation) requiring modifications to the fuel system. A number of tight clearances such as high kerbs required the frequent replacement of scuffed and cracked plastic skirt panels. Dave Allinson, a specialist coachbuilder, was employed on a part time basis for this task. After some eighteen months' service, the new Carlyle bodied Darts were ordered as more robust vehicles. When these replacements arrived for routes R1/R11, Roundabout's MRL fleet was dispersed within Selkent during August 1990; three to BX for the last days of Bexleybus and ten to TB.

History of the Darts (DT)

Vehicle specifications:

Chassis: Dennis Dart 8SDL

Engine: Cummins 6BT 5.9 litre

Bodywork: Carlyle 28 seats

In 1990 Selkent was looking to implement a midibus network for the Bromley area and several routes were earmarked for conversion, such as the busy route 126. With this in mind, Selkent participated in a massive London Buses group order with the bodybuilder Duple for the brand new 'Dennis Dart'. This concept had every expectation of creating a robust small bus, replacing the early generations of midibuses. The Dart project brought together the expertise of Dennis Specialist Vehicles, combined with the Cummins engine and Allison gearbox so successfully applied to the Metrorider, plus a stylish "Dartline" body by Duple, the bodybuilder of some seventy years experience.

The first twenty-seven Darts were duly delivered to London United, whereupon Duple rather abruptly sold out to Plaxton. The new owners decided to cease production of the Dartline body, selling the design rights to the rather smaller bodybuilder, Carlyle of Edgbaston. The name Carlyle was synonymous with provincial "bread van" conversions and production of bodies for the Ford Transit and Freight Sherpa. Incidentally, in 1989, five Sherpa conversions were to find their way to Roundabout, to replace RHs and an MRL loaned to Bexleybus during a spate of mechanical problems at BX.

Production of the originally specified Dartline body was an exciting and proud time for Carlyle, with the prospect of this larger bus body yielding considerable remunerative opportunities for this small company. This euphoria was demonstrated when their first bus, DT 28, rolled off the production line in April 1990 bearing the name "Pride of Carlyle". The vehicle was delivered in "all-over" red, and whilst at Plumstead for inspection, had its grey skirt and "ROUNDABOUT" regalia applied, before being allocated to OB. Interestingly, the second body produced by Carlyle was paired with DT55, which after initial delivery to TB, found its way to OB in Spring 1991.

DT28's first public outing was in late April, when it was entered into the Southampton UK Coach Rally, winning the category of Best Dual Purpose Vehicle. Bryan Constable drove and Peter o' Rourke (Selkent's private hire manager) navigated, with Selkent Travel's finest polishes and cloths contained in a large red steel box, complete with "hops" logo, carried onboard! The coach seats were fitted with headrest covers embroidered with the ROUNDABOUT logo.

A courtesy service in May 1990 from Orpington to a local fete at Broke Hill Golf Club, near Hewitt's Farm, was DT28's passenger carrying debut. This was an opportunity to show off the eye-catching, flamboyant curved front end, and contributed to a boost in the image of the small bus, with the icing on the cake being the inscription "Pride of Carlyle". Internally, DT28 was fitted with high backed coach seats, which rendered it suitable for deployment in the Selkent Travel fleet. However, the DT interiors incorporated many of the recommendations of the Disabled Persons Transport Advisory Committee (DiPTAC). Black and yellow chevrons marked step edges and changes in gangway heights, thicker, green dimpled handrails featured, and an internal "bus stopping" sign provided. Selkent wished to lead the way in implementing these specifications, and while its Titan fleet was capable of modification, it was decided the best course of action to introduce these features at Roundabout was by means of allocating the first Dart deliveries to OB. The first thirteen Selkent Darts (DT28-41) were thus sent to work on routes R1/R11. Roundabout's displaced MRLs were mostly reallocated to TB, in time to commence the 14th July 1990 Bromley midibus network (routes 126 / 314 / 336 / 396) pending further deliveries of new midibuses.

Above: As the fleet showbus, DT28 attended many local events, such as the 1990 Bexley Show. "Pride of Carlyle" is seen carrying its original registration, plus fog lights and large driving mirrors, features "borrowed" from DT168 whilst at OB for MoT preparations.

Below: Rail Replacement was an occasional part of Roundabout's remit, as seen working alongside Selkent's sister low cost unit, Bexleybus. DT29 & L265 await the next train at Bexley station during 1990. *Photos: D. Hulls*

The Dennis Dart was at the time the largest midibus used by LBL, and at 8.5metres, was the maximum length that a midibus driver with a class 3 licence could drive.

However DT29/41 departed to London United after only about a year's service, during spring 1991. So with just 11 DT for a PVR of 13 for the R1/R11, a twelfth arrived in the shape of DT55, which transferred from Bromley garage. For some reason the DT class did not stay long at TB and their batch moved over to London United. In 1992, two DTs received Routemaster cherished registrations following conversion of Selkent's last crew route 36B. DT28 was originally registered G28 TGW, and became 49 CLT (once carried by RM1049), and DT55 originally G55 TGW, became WLT 575 (once carried by RM575). It may be noted that another former route 36B Routemaster cherished plate, VLT 240 (from RM240), was transferred to the prototype Titan T1131 at TB around this time, before being assigned to DT32.

High backed coach seats in maroon and grey moquette were fitted to DT55 as well as DT28 from new, while DT30 & DT31 were similarly fitted out from two DTs due to be reallocated from TB.

During April 1992, braking retarders were fitted to the fleet. DT45 was loaned from TB for a month whilst the DTs were modified, before being sent on to TL.

In late August 1992, DT32 on route R11, was stolen by youths from outside Queen Marys hospital whilst the driver was away.

It was discovered having crashed into a tree at Culverstone Green near Vigo. As the wreck of DT32 arrives back at base, Andy Ewing picks up the pieces as Jack "John" Reidy looks on in disbelief!
Photo: A. Blackburn

The decision was made to carry out a complete front end rebuild, which was undertaken by Marshalls of Cambridge, Carlyle having been bought out a year earlier. DT32 reappeared in March 1993 with a new style front blind box later sporting the registration VLT 240.

Rebuilt DT32 prior to fitment of its cherished registration, seen here in spring 1993, temporarily expired in Mickelham Road, St Pauls Cray, whilst on route R1.
Photo: G. Walker

Privatisation of Selkent in September 1994 saw OB's Dart fleet sanded down and resprayed into overall red livery, with "Stagecoach Selkent" names above the door/drivers cab, while large *"ROUNDABOUT"* fleetnames were reapplied to the sides.

Upon closure of OB, four Roundabout DTs (32/34/35/37) were being utilised on the 1995 Bromley Park and Ride service. Many of the remainder were sent to Catford (TL) to upgrade route 124 from Mercedes (MW) operation. Some also appeared at Plumstead (PD) for routes 177 / 306. DT32 stayed a while longer at TB and was used on the 336 during 1996, and observed on one occasion on route 320, no doubt deputising for a Titan falling victim to the challenges of Stock Hill!

The Carlyle Darts gave exemplary service at OB, so it is perhaps churlish to mention that they were lacking in just one Roundabout "tradition": maybe by oversight or perhaps consciously so, they were never christened with individual names! In keeping with the MRL sentiment to perpetuate bird names by using the "II" suffix, the author wonders if, for example, "Sparrow III" might have been considered?

History of the Mercedes Carlyle (MC)

Engine: Mercedes 3.64 litre

Chassis: Mercedes Benz 811D

Bodywork: Carlyle 28 seats

The Mercedes 811D chassis had been more usually paired with bodies by Alexander (MA class), but In July 1989, a Carlyle body was mounted on a 811D chassis for evaluation purposes. This demonstrator, F430 BOP, was trialled by Selkent and worked from Catford Garage over routes L3 and 181. The vehicle appeared in red livery with grey skirt, but with a white band below the windows, similar to the Starrider fleet. The livery was complimented with "Catford Cat" emblems over the wheel arches. F430 BOP was awarded fleet number MC1.

It performed well, and the neat bodywork with large, clear, rectangular blind box impressed Selkent, which purchased the vehicle and officially brought MC1 into stock in April 1990. Four further MCs became available as a result of a speculative batch constructed at Carlyle. These were purchased at a bargain price as replacements for the ex-LCNW automatic transmission OVs, which were proving to lack power and were clearly tired and worn. MC2/3/5 entered service on route R3 in August 1990, followed by MC4, which was fitted with an unusually long blind for use at both OB and TB. Seating was finished in "red diamond" moquette, and DiPTAC lime green handrails were installed.

In December 1990, MCs 2-5 were sent to Catford garage for use on Lewisham local "Centrelink" festive special services, returning to OB and route R3 in the newyear. In April 1991, MC1 had her "Catford Cat" motifs painted out and sent to join her sisters at OB as the spare bus for route R3, sadly for Austin Blackburn, who had designed the artwork for these emblems whilst at Selkent HQ years earlier!

During summer 1993, all five had their Mercedes gearboxes replaced with a new Allison AT545 type, and from November they underwent full refurbishment at Marshalls of Cambridge, with MC3 the first to be treated. One downside of the knockdown price was the lack of spray chrome underseal lining, necessitating replacement of floor components and skirting panels, with the original brown saloon flooring being pulled up and a fresh grey floor laid down. Whilst the refurbishments were taking place, glued rather than riveted body panels led to large areas of body sections breaking away in an effort to replace individual damaged panels.

MC4 occasionally saw use on loan to Bromley (TB) on Sundays on route 161, making good use of its extra long blind display. For most of its life with Roundabout, MC4 carried RM cherished number plate WLT 400, while MC1 was similarly treated to WLT 491 for a time.

All five served to the last day of Roundabout operations, and on the night of 1st December 1995, they were swiftly despatched to Catford (TL) for use on route 124 and 273, initiating replacement of the allocation of unloved of Mercedes (MW) vehicles. Shortly before leaving OB, the cherished number plates were removed, however, their original registrations were not sent for, and they left for TL carrying rather inconsistent index marks.

MC1 with original registration (the first of three!) and Catford Cat emblem at Catford Bridge stand awaiting passengers for route L3 on 6th June 1990. *Photo: Julian Smith*

MC1, when carrying cherished RM number plate WLT 491, finds plenty of custom at Orpington Station on 5th August 1992.
Photo: K. Gurney

MC4 wearing WLT 400. This plate was transferred from Daf Optare Delta DA1, and prior to that was carried on a route 36B Routemaster. Walnuts centre, 5th April 1993.
Photo: K. Gurney

The FMs: a Royal Connection

Chassis: Iveco 49.10

Engine: Iveco 2.45 litre

Bodywork: Marshall 23 seats

As part of the November 1992 Orpington network changes, and with the remaining RH class at OB beginning to show their age, the decision was made to order 10 new Iveco midibuses for use on the R2/R4/R5/R6/R8, with an element of spares. As Carlyle had closed down their business, many midibus body orders throughout the UK were met by Marshalls.

At their Cambridge factory, Marshalls also had a sixty year Aerospace reputation. In the Spring of 1993, HRH Prince Charles was visiting Marshalls on Queen's Flight business, when he noticed the first FMs (1/9/10) complete and awaiting collection. Bryan Constable was also visiting on business, and overheard the distinct voice of The Prince of Wales comment "Ooh! My boys would *love* one of those to play with!" as HRH passed the FM production line. The Princes William and Harry have not been available for comment(!), but when the FM class was shown off to the press at Langley Park on 7th May, all ten vehicles succeeded in turning up! With hindsight, perhaps FM1 should have been given the pet name "William" or "Harry" at the naming ceremony on 31st July!

Prince Charles inspects the FM production line at Marshalls.

Spring 1993

Photo: Marshalls of Cambridge

Even before entering service, the FM class was clearly enjoying some celebrity status. FM1 won the distinguished 'Bus of the Year' award, with OB driver Richard Stephens picking up 'Driver of the Year', at the Brighton Coach Show on 25th April 1993.

Then on 7th May, the whole fleet of ten was driven to the former LT Sports & Social Club at Langley Park for a photo opportunity. "FM" stood for "Ford Marshall". The Ford involvement was disputed, in particular by Austin Blackburn, Roundabout's Engineering Foreman, for the simple reason that there were no Ford components on the vehicles. Iveco no longer sustained a UK dealership, and therefore entrusted Ford to "hard sell" this new product. Consequently, Austin had removed the blue "Ford" badges from the radiator grills of all ten vehicles, only to be instructed to re-attach them for the purposes of the trade presence at the press launch!

Unfortunately, not all the badges could be found, so a Ford sales executive was despatched with all speed to KT at Sidcup to purchase some replacements whilst the photoshoot was postponed for almost an hour! FM10 *(opposite, photo by K. Gurney)* is shown having her "Ford" badge hastily replaced. Needless to say, the badges were swiftly removed afterwards!

Even the number plates had to be scrupulously devoid of any dealer's name, so the plates supplied by "Gilbert Rice of Cambridge" as fitted by Marshalls had to be replaced. Such memorabilia appeared on sale at the LOTS Fayre later in 1994: the rear plate of FM4 now adorns the author's bedroom!

All ten FMs numerically lined-up for the camera at Langley Park, 25th April 1993.
Photo: K.Gurney

FM 1/9/10 entered service at OB, in early May, with their sisters introduced progressively throughout the month.

The FM class served the Orpington network well, despite only surviving for little over two and a half years. Being the last batch of brand new vehicles delivered to Roundabout, they were relatively unworn upon withdrawal, and a few can still be found to this day with small independents in the far flung corners of the UK.

The original 'Rising Star' concept was in some small measure realised in the FM class, as a result of being named after constellations. However, it is only possible to make this perhaps frivolous observation with the benefit of hindsight, for back in 1993, the significance of stars was unknown: a safely guarded secret only revealed during research for this publication!

FM1 & 10 parked facing the shutters at OB on 2nd October 1994, with blinds set for more unusual duties! *Photo: Tom Gurney*

THE GALLERY

A1 on route R1, 28th November 1987 (above) approaches Orpington Memorial, in a very typical 1980s suburban social scene, as displayed by a well dressed elderly gentleman in matching tweed attire, and a mother overseeing her daughter's early days of learning to ride a 'fairy' bike. RH18 "Sandpiper" appears well laden in the opposite direction! Ten days later, A1 on route R3 (below) quietly follows Metrobus Olympian UWW 13X on route 61 through Orpington High Street 8th December 1987. *Photos: K.Gurney*

RH3 "Puffin" on route R5 leads A1 on route R6 out towards the country lanes of rural Orpington. Spur Road, 23rd December 1987. Maroon "E" plate stickers feature on this dual bus and Green Line coach stop, just visible above RH3. *Photo: K. Gurney.*

RH9 "Heron" seen here after circumnavigating the roundabout at Orpington War Memorial, on the R7, which was the only route to perform this unusual manoeuvre. 16th April 1991. *Photo: Julian Smith.*

OV4 "Chinook" waits in the middle of Station Square, Petts Wood, for further custom, 28th August 1987. The problem with car parking at the time can be seen: it would be very rare to find a bus parked against the kerb at this location, until the bus stand was extended and made a clearway a year later.

A fine morning on Poverest Road brings OV 49 pausing for custom on its hail-and-ride section, as the driver of OV 26 stops for a chat with his "leader". 27th June 1990.
Photos: K. Gurney

Sisters wearing old and new liveries pass each other at Tescos, Foots Cray, 30th June 1990. Britbus produced a model of E642 KYW "Sparrow II" which was one of the last in the fleet to lose maroon and grey.

Crown Lane Spur on Sunday 4th March 1990, before route 208 was extended Petts Wood – Orpington on Sundays. Passengers needed to change here for a connecting R11 to reach Orpington. T420, a recent arrival at TB from London Forest district, seems to have no driver relief (judging by its destination display) and proceeds to Bromley Garage, overtaking "Teal II" on stand. *Photos: K. Gurney*

DT35 pulls in at the old Nugent Industrial Estate stop, as a postman among other intending passengers prepare to board an already crowded R1 journey. 18th August 1991. *Photo: K. Gurney*

During her final days in service with Roundabout, DT32 parked up on the Queen Mary's Hospital overspill stand between R11 journeys on 25th October 1995. This bus was selected for early release to TB for the 1995 festive Bromley Park & Ride contract, as shown by the advertising already in place. *Photo: Andrew Jeffreys*

A quartet of MCs and an FM proudly sit side-by-side below the Selkent hops banner adorning unit 5 in January 1994. *Photo: Tom Gurney*

Brand new MC5 positions herself behind Boroline 915, a former Dundee Ailsa on the Tesco courtesy T1 service, with Plumstead's T748 parked up between route 161 journeys on the other sideof Station Square, Petts Wood. 31st August 1990. *Photo: K. Gurney*

Whilst on route R8, FM1 "Capricorn", with Stagecoach logo applied, meets up with Dunton Green's AN192 on route 493 at Orpington Station. The Atlantean was a London & Country vehicle, but by this time the route was operated by LondonLinks.
Photo: K. Gurney

FM4 "Aries" picks up a passenger along the former "Hail and Ride" section of route R4, close to the old St Mary Cray Police Station. This was also the location where drivers would change over, just a stone's throw from OB. 21st October 1995. *Photo: A. Jeffreys*

In between showers, the "Catford Cat" (above the front wheelarch) on this Starrider stalks new prey in Orpington! On a brief loan to OB, prior to taking up allocation at TL on the new midi-bus network based there, SR60 finds herself on route R1 on 29th June 1989.

MA4, nearing its terminus at Green Street Green on route R11, was a vehicle destined for replacement of Routemasters as "Gold Arrow" midibus routes 28 & 31 in west London, after a period of bedding-in with Roundabout, as seen in March 1989. *Photos: K.Gurney*

A FRIEND IN NEED.......
Selkent's low cost units became friends indeed! Above, former Roundabout RH21 "Gannet", in her new guise as Bexleybus 74, plays "Chase Me Charlie" on route R3 with OV2 "Hurricane", 24th June 1988.

Centre: "Nightingale II" in Roundabout livery helped out for several months in 1989, seen at Eltham Church on 15th August, leading a trio of B16s.

Below: Helping out at OB a year later, an example of the new triaxle midibus product by Talbot Pullman is trialled on route R7. Petts Wood, 23rd June 1990. The vehicle carries a Warwickshire registration, with no other clues to its origin!
Photos: K. Gurney

A gallery of visiting variety shows: (above) a Sherpa in Manchester Minibuses livery on route R4 leading OV4 "Chinook" on route R3 in Orpington High Street 29th June 1989; (below left) a very rare Mercedes / AMI vehicle, G495 FFA, trialled on route R3, seen in Petts Wood on 28th August 1990, one of a very small number with a body built by a cottage industry in The Potteries; while soon after (below), another British bus body builder ventured into the midibus market with this Portsdown Dart by Wadham Stringer, trialled on the Peckham midibus network, using its innovative dot matrix blind display, although during its stay at Roundabout, G895 XPX made use of an ordinary OB roller blind placed in the windscreen!

Photos top and above left: K. Gurney; above right: Tom Gurney

Britibus' excellent 1:78 model of MRL66 "Sparrow II".

OV1 "Typhoon" and MRL66 "Sparrow II" in a classic pose on the Green Street Green stand while drivers enjoy a chat, 24th June 1988 (above). Three months later, OV1 (minus a section of her rear window!) finds herself making a smoky departure from Petts Wood while Boroline 276, a Bedford YMT, waits with the Tesco courtesy service on 30th September 1988 (below). *Photos: K. Gurney*

Above: At peak times, the Orpington Station stand often found a group of RHs keeping each other company, such as RH15 "Kingfisher", RH1 "Kestrel" and RH5 "Owl", in spring 1992. This trio would have interworked between routes R2 and R5. *Photo: Tom Gurney*

ROUNDABOUT'S FIRST MONTH: black & white studies by E.L. Collinson

Above: RH24 "Seagull" passes a Coal Post in Cudham Lane on route R5.

Centre: RH17 "Snipe" driven by Eric Cormack as he trundles through Farnborough village on route R1.

Below: RH10 "Wren" and OV5 "Whirlwind" at Orpington Station prepare to set out on their country journeys on routes R5 and R6 respectively.

Above: An FM line-up at Unit 5 under the Selkent banner in January 1994, with BL85 just visible far left. *Photo: Tom Gurney*

Above left: RH22 formerly "Hawk" came out of repaint as "Heron", a regular performer on route R2, resting at Petts Wood in Spring 1994. *Photo: Dave Gurney.*

Above right: Just a few days after it was announced in spring 1995 that Roundabout was to close, RH1 "Kestrel" is seen "mechanical" on route R8 at Orpington station. Bus and driver appear sad at their predicament. *Photo: Tom Gurney*

Left: MC3 appearing unusually on route R2, in the late evening sunshine, Orpington High Street, July 1994. *Photo: Tom Gurney*

Snowfall in early February 1992 brought inevitable disruption, but Roundabout battled through. Above, a pair of Darts on route R1 led by DT35 pass Bromley Garage, 7th February. Below, taking care not to join in the tobogganing, RH2 "Robin" gingerly picks her way down Tubbenden Lane on route R4, 9th February. *Photos: K. Gurney*

Above: OV38 on route R3 and L91 in LBL compliant livery: red with grey skirt and white lining, side-by-side in Station Square. The Olympian driver is expecting a relief after this 161 trip to Woolwich, evidenced by "Plumstead Garage" following the ampersand on the destination blind. 8th June 1990.

Below: the 20 minute headway on route R3 matched the train service at Petts Wood station, and with a visible presence on stand, succeeded in attracting substantial volumes of homegoing commuters. MC3 with the 1820 departure, boards one warm June evening in 1994. *Photos: K. Gurney*

DT28 "Pride of Carlyle" presents herself on her regular R11 beat in Orpington High Street 11ᵗʰ September 1992, soon after being allocated the cherished number plate of RM 1049.

Photo: K. Gurney

In Roundabout's final months, vehicle allocation became rather mixed, such as FMs on route R1, DTs on the R3, and MCs on the R4, etc., so it came as no surprise to find DT55 at the Pallant Way stand on route R4. Cherished number plate from RM 575 was later allocated to East London Trident 17260.
Photo: A. Jeffreys

DT36 became one of the last Roundabout Darts to be painted into Stagecoach "all over" red, seen on route R1 in January 1995 just before transformation. Just a year after delivery, DT36 required extensive front end rebuild following a serious accident. Unlike a similar fate befalling DT32, DT36 emerged with her original appearance intact.
Photo: K. Gurney

LITTLE BUS MEETS BIG BUS!

Above: in early 1988, roads works closed part of Orpington High Street, and the one way gyratory including Goodmead Road became two-way; hence RH6 "Swift" on route R4 appears to be heading the wrong way! Route 208 terminated at the 493 stand, as depicted by TB's T1115. 27th January 1988.

Below: in the company of three New Cross Titans on route 21, the most recent addition to the Roundabout fleet, F197 YDA, awaiting its "M97 Seagull II" decals, appears humbled as she departs Tesco on 25th November 1988. The double run via the new superstore had been introduced on routes R1 & R11 the previous July. *Photos: K. Gurney*

Providing a Friendly Service

At the Sharp End

A bus service's ambassador is its driver. The person who interfaces with the public conveys the company image and is responsible for shaping the mindset of his/her passengers. From the outset, it was clear that the new style, localised bus service, required the altruistic touch achieved by staff "willing to go the extra mile". The 1986 publicity told us that the 'Roundabouts' and their drivers will be friendly additions to our native scene and would be a welcome sight for all.

Roundabout's pledge was fulfilled, as there were several drivers who really did make the effort; genuine characters whom passengers got to know, as drivers tended to stay on the same route and shift every week. Drivers therefore became familiar with passenger boarding and alighting habits, so on hail-and-ride routes, regulars, to their delight, were often automatically picked up and set down exactly where they wanted, where practical, even outside their own homes!

The appreciation of passengers could be measured in the volume of sweets, apples, and cans of drinks eagerly handed to drivers. Clearly, a Roundabout bus was a happy bus in the eyes of the "punters". Rarely have we heard of problems of rowdiness, and assault screens were deemed unnecessary until fitted fleetwide simply as a matter of routine.

The People who made it happen

Local service with local people; the staff of Roundabout were all generally local men and women who often used to walk to work, but some made use of the N47 night bus, a route that in the early days only had a handful of journeys along Cray Avenue. Ian Jones, who was there from day one with Roundabout, and who is still a driver on the "R" network now with Metrobus, always maintained he only joined for a laugh! It must have been a good time, because he continues doing the job he enjoys, albeit with a much tougher operating territory and stricter industry.

There was a great feeling amongst staff, being such a small garage everyone knew each other and swapping duties was seen as no problem, and the management / staff relations were very well balanced with no real issues at a local level.

Smiles galore in Petts Wood! The first journey of new route R7, OV4 'Chinook' driven by Pat Carter, perhaps just as excited as some of the punters about to enjoy a 'special service' to new areas of Orpington, such as the Coppice Estate.
Photo: K. Gurney

The author's favourite bus "Sandpiper II" on route R1 rounds the corner from Crown Lane Spur into Bromley Common. Driver Dave Bird waves to the seven year old photographer daringly standing against a traffic island amidst the busy A21 one bright autumnal day in 1989.
Photo: Tom Gurney

Christmas 1986, and Kevin Lawler brings some tinsel and festive high spirits to the R3. A couple of years later, one or two RHs were festooned with mini Christmas trees complete with lights connected to the dashboard!
Photo: K.Gurney

Above left: David Hulls: Bus Driver of the Year, snapped at the Bromley Park & Ride town terminus a year later. *Photo: K.Gurney. Above right:* Austin Blackburn, Workshop Foreman, at his desk in the Unit 5 Engineering Office during 1992. *Photo: A. Blackburn*

THE DRIVERS' ROOM AT UNIT 17

THE EARLY DAYS

Top left: "Boris"

Top right: Brian Connolly

Bottom left: Pat Carter and John Payne

Photos supplied by Paul Bishop

153

Everybody jumps in to shift immobilised OV4 at Petts Wood Station Square. *Left to right: Ian Speller, Vic Sharpe, Vince Simpson and Barry Philpott.* 5th December 1989.   Photo: *K.Gurney*

A rare opportunity to meet a group of Roundabout drivers at the FM presentation ceremony, Langley Park, 7th May 1993. *Left to right: Martin Edwards, Arthur Harper, Lyn Morrel, Ivor Thornton, Dave Lye, Ray Wells, Vic Sharpe, Eric Cormack, Roy Sewell (General Manager). Photo: K.Gurney*

Charity Bus Pull 1989

Photo: Courtesy "News Shopper"

To quote from the "Going Your Way" booklet, "Drivers will soon become fully fledged local characters". Indeed, during 1989, a team of Roundabout drivers helped raise funds for the Brook Hospital Cardiac Unit by staging a "bus pull". An MRL was tugged along the R11 route from Queen Marys Hospital to Orpington Memorial. In the photograph above, Penny Baldock was at the wheel, while among those flexing their muscles in the interests of charity were Brian Connolly, Paul Bishop, Chris Saunders, Kevin Lawler, and a regular R4 passenger who worked for British Rail. Around £700 was raised en route.

A selection of drivers' memories

"My RH came to the rescue after heavy snow had fallen. I was on route R2, when on reaching Downe village, I saw the postman had got stuck in the snow drift. Without too much effort, I pushed his van along the lanes.....the bumper of a Robin Hood is perfect for the job! I later became the regular R5 late turn, after which I had the exciting task of shuttling as many buses as I could for refuelling at Ruxley before signing off! Through working beside the engineers, I became interested in their roles and with Austin's encouragement, I trained as a fitter at TL, and eventually became night engineer at TB"

WAI WONG

"There was one occasion on the R5 when my bus was picking up more than the usual number of regular passengers for the trip. What was even more unusual was that they all alighted at Orpington station. I secured my bus and then went to use the 'offices' on platform 5. On returning to the bus, I found an envelope on the Wayfayrer and a box on the first seat behind the cab. I opened the envelope to find a birthday card, and on checking the box found a birthday cake. To this day I don't know how they knew it was my birthday, but the cake was yummy."

DAVID HULLS.

"I was actually the General Manager and I went out many times to drive the buses (best part of the job!), I also recall covering some engineering shifts and helping out with the night time fuelling."

ADRIAN JONES

"Ask anyone who was there on day one and I think the most memorable thing was that every road you went down and every corner that you turned were so many photographers.....even on step ladders on the roundabout".

DON MARGETTS

"What was supposed to be a mission to just help out for a few months on loan at Orpington, worked out to be six years as Roundabout's workshop foreman, but it was a great six years".

AUSTIN BLACKBURN

"I only joined for a dare, and I needed some new clothes (uniform)!"   **IAN JONES**

"I was driving RH8 'Swan' on the M25 on my way to start my journey on route 22. I was following a Army truck full of soldiers all pointing and jeering. I instantly thought they were laughing at me in my little bus, but they were pointing out that smoke was billowing out from my engine bay! I pulled up and got on to my controller via the ever useful RACAL Vodafone appliance. However out on the motorway, I was out of range of signal, and so in the dark, I trampled through muddy fields in the direction of Dunton Green garage to borrow their telephone. A very muddy pair of shoes and trousers indeed!"

PAUL BISHOP

"After a period of time working at Catford garage driving Starrider's on their midibus network, the opportunity to transfer over to Roundabout interested me, particularly as it would be free from working Sundays. However as an' auto' licence holder I found myself route bound to the R1/R11 MRLs, until I took my manual test in a yellow and red Sherpa at the Plumstead training school, to enable me to drive the OV/RH fleet at OB."

CHRIS PERRY

Changeover Points

When the time came for a driver to be relieved, passengers could wait with "excitement" to greet the new character about to convey them further! R1/R11 changed drivers in Cray Avenue beside Nugent Estate for a 30 second walk to the garage. On the bridge over the Cray some 400 metres further south, drivers on route R3 (and later R2) would effect a changeover, cheerfully "moaning" what a nice day it was for the five minute walk beside the river. On wet and windy days however, they frequently sprinted towards Cray Avenue to hastily flag down colleague on a passing route R1/R11! On the opposite side of the River Cray, R4 changed drivers near the old Victorian St Mary Cray police station building, also a short walk from OB.

The R7 changed drivers in Orpington High Street after circumnavigating the War Memorial roundabout: the only route to backtrack 180 degrees. Nothing has since repeated this practice. The R2/R5/R6 changed drivers at Orpington Station, sometimes neatly parking beside the preserved semaphore signal in the turning circle, as the RHs and FMs were small enough not to cause an obstruction to their larger counterparts. The author wonders what happened to that signal, which was whisked away when the new interchange was built?

"ON TIME ALL THE TIME" *(below)* **one side of the 1994 Duty Card for duty 35 route R1.**

R 1			BROMLEY COMMON & SIDCUP QUEEN MARYS HOSP					T.S.: 19			DUTY: 35

MON - FRI   31 5 1994   D.S.: 23   OB GARAGE   OPO

TRIP NO	PREV DUTY	BUS NO	BCOM CR S	FRNB GR	GSTG GR	ORPN WM■	SMCY CI	SMCY SN	SPCY MY	SPCY GR S	NEXT DUTY
85	26	1					1202	1204	1211	1214	
109		1	1306	1314	1318	1323	1332	1334	1341	1344	
133		1	1436	1444	1448	1453	1502	SHOW SPCY GR S			37

TRIP NO	PREV DUTY	BUS NO	BCOM CR S	FRNB GR	GSTG QH	GSTG GR	ORPN HP	ORPN WM■	SMCY CI	SMCY SN	SPCY MY	SPCY GR S	SPCY GR	FOOT PO	SIDC HP S
149	14	5							1602	1604	1611	1614			
173		5	1706	1714		1718		1723	1732	1734	1741	1744			
197		5	1836	1844		1848		1852	1859	1901	1906		1909	___	1915
211		5	2012	2020	2024	2025	2029	2033	2040	2042	2047			2052	2058

BUSES RUN DEAD ON JOURNEYS UNDERLINED   TAKE OVER TIMES
RESTRICTIONS   1202 1602
■ = QSI POINT

ON TIME ALL THE TIME

Topping Up the Mileage:

Routes 22 / 23 / 26 / 401H / D1

With the new Orpington network bedding in nicely, by the Autumn of 1986 Roundabout looked at expanding operations outside Greater London, with an eye on routes serving the small Darenth valley villages on behalf of the local authority. Orpington Buses Ltd successfully tendered for route 401H: a Kent County Council (KCC) Sunday only service linking the scenic villages of Eynsford and Farningham with the Darenth Valley hospital near Dartford. This service began on 26th October 1986, ideally utilising a coach seated Iveco (RH), carrying running number OB24, with one round trip from Eynsford Station. However passenger loadings were not as anticipated, and route 401H proved uneconomic. The route was withdrawn on 17th May 1987. The small narrow lanes in Lullingstone were traversed for empty garage runs, allowing for a spectacular crossing of the River Darenth ford at Eynsford.

Regular 401H driver "Boris" takes RH11 "Sparrow" for a splash through the River Darenth ford at Eynsford village, May 1987. Oblivious to the maritime activity, the passenger remains stuck with her head in a Sunday paper! *Photo: A. Jeffreys.*

However, all was not lost and a fresh look at KCC work was once again trialled. Owing to the fact that the bulk of Roundabout work finished by about 1900 daily, it was identified that some vehicles could be assigned to additional work outside the area during the periods they would otherwise remain idle in the garage.

In spring 1987, a tender block issued by KCC for some Sevenoaks area Monday to Saturday evening services was won by Roundabout from Transcity. From 30th May 1987, routes 22 (Sevenoaks - Tonbridge), 23 (Westerham - Sevenoaks) and 26 (Sevenoaks – Seal – Kemsing – Otford circular) became worked by two Iveco RHs, thus rounding off the daytime services run commercially by Kentish Bus.

One duty involved running empty to Sevenoaks for the half hour live route 22 trip to Tonbridge, followed by a swift return to Sevenoaks. The blinds were then changed for the route 26 trip to Shoreham, rounding off the evening with a short run light through the lanes via Chelsfield to OB.

Snapped through the OB office window, Paul Bishop prepares RH8 "Swan" for their evening duty light run to Sevenoaks. He proudly points to his homemade blind for the handful of evening journeys on route 22. *Photo: courtesy P. Bishop*

However, KCC saw fit to reissue tenders for these evening services a matter of months later. As a result, from 16th January 1988, Roundabout lost the 23 to Kentish Bus while Transcity won back the 26. Route 22 was retained by Roundabout, however, after a further few months KCC withdrew funding for route 22, which was consequently discontinued after 8th October 1988.

Around the same time, maroon and grey even appeared in central London. The London Docklands Development Corporation (LDDC) funded a single evening journey on route D1 from the Isle of Dogs to London Bridge Station, after conclusion of the daytime service by East London (using LS vehicles in a red and white livery from West Ham garage). Roundabout was awarded the work, which was performed off the second-half "R2 school bus duty". An RH would operate the 1540 ex-Biggin Hill Valley, which by Charles Darwin School was loaded full to the door with schoolchildren. On arrival at Orpington Station, the lengthy light run to Docklands was made via Rotherhithe Tunnel. A group of "City Big-wigs" formed the regular clientele taken along Commercial Road and over London Bridge. This curious route was fairly short-lived, being withdrawn after 3rd March 1989, but it was an interesting variant to Roundabout's otherwise localised network.

In Spring 1987, RH11 "Sparrow" passes through Farningham village en route to Eynsford on the short-lived 401H service.

Photo: A. Jeffreys

Private Hires: Keeping the fleet immaculate

When costings were being drawn up as part of the Rising Star team's response to tendering, the possibilities of private hire work was investigated. Bryan's prospectus stated "Budgeted income from this is deliberately cautious. If this work increases as is hoped then the company's growth will be that much greater." With need to keep one vehicle as breakdown cover, a second to cover for accident damage, and a third as a routine maintenance spare, there was no slack during Monday to Friday daytimes to accept such work. However, at weekends, four vehicles could be identified as surplus to operational requirements on Saturdays, and eleven on Sundays. Bryan estimated that charging £70 per day, for a hire involving a 90-mile round trip, would net a profit of £22, resulting in an annual profit of £3,800. This was based on a guarantee of two private hires each Saturday throughout the year, and four Sunday bookings during the summer months. The abundance of pub darts teams in St Mary Cray convinced Bryan of the certainty of private hire! Consequently, the order for the Robin Hood fleet had included three vehicles to coach specification. RH1 "Kestrel", RH23 "Hawk" and RH24 "Seagull" were duly delivered with high backed seats and deeper upholstery in a red and orange striped moquette. Bryan also asked Optare's Russell Richardson to produce something special on some of the OV fleet, and OV 3/4/5 were delivered with "superior" seating.

The "Going Your Way" booklet informed the public that "Rent-a-Roundabout" was a serious consideration, thus emphasising that the 'new little buses' would not only prove useful on stage carriage bus work, but also as private hire vehicles.

Again the message was conveyed by means of a cartoon image depicting with what appears to be some students dressed up for a school prom, complete with bow ties and balloons in tow!

In practice, many school outings were to places such as the popular animal centre at Godstone Farm, and children's birthday parties to theme parks. The drivers too arranged their own evenings out on behalf of local social and leisure clubs, with west end Christmas lights tours proving popular. The use of crisp white linen head rest covers ("antimacassars") positioned neatly over each seatback, and bearing the embroidered maroon Roundabout fleetname, complimented the private chartered ambiance onboard perfectly.

In 1988, three of Roundabout's MRLs (74-76) were delivered to coach specification to maintain this successful secondary activity. It was now possible to offer both a 33 seat vehicle as well as a 21 seat "minicoach" hire facility. RH1 'Kestrel' (easily capable of speeds of 70mph) and MRL74 'Gannet II' were maintained to an exceptionally high standard and kept immaculate for such purposes, and the latter even sported chrome wheel trims! Bryan's interest in the Brighton Coach Show often resulted in these prestigious examples making a trip to the south coast! All three MRLs were often assigned private hire duties on Saturdays, resulting in RH or OV appearances on routes R1/R11.

Upon arrival of the 28 seater Dennis Darts at Orpington, "Gannet II" and "Woodpecker II" moved to Bromley garage for routes 126/314/336/396. In being subjected to harsher operating territory, vandalism and general cleanliness of their interiors took a downturn on these once impeccable members of the Roundabout fleet. However, with private hire bookings for 33 seaters still being received, the decision was made to utilise Plumstead's MT6. Bodied by Reeve Burgess, this 33 seater was intended for driver training purposes at Catford, but was delivered with a number of "quality features", making it suitable for private hire work. It was later renumbered MTL6 to reflect its unique higher seating capacity compared to its mobility bus counterparts. MTL6 never ran from OB; instead drivers had to make their own way to Plumstead and work the private hire from there: a clear sign that Selkent Travel did not want to lose sight of their prestigious vehicle, reportedly much admired by the private hire manager. Indeed, it carried cherished registration number VLT 77.

Later DT28 'Pride of Carlyle' became a member of the OB private hire fleet, although with just RH1/DT28/DT55 (21 & 28 seaters) now to choose from, charter bookings dropped away somewhat. The MRLs had been the backbone of Roundabout's private hire venture and certainly were missed in this role.

ROUNDABOUT FLEET LIST (permanent & semi-permanent vehicles)

Livery Codes: BB - Bexleybus; CB - Chelsea blue; EB - Eastbourne Buses;
M&G - Maroon & grey; R - Red; R&W - Red & white

FLEET NO.	NAME	REG. NO.	CHASSIS	BODY	SEATING LAYOUT	ORIGINAL LIVERY	LATER LIVERIES
RH 1	Kestrel	C501 DYM	Iveco Daily 49-10	Robin Hood	DP21F	M&G	R; M&G
RH2	Robin	C502 DYM			B21F	M&G	R
RH3	Puffin	C503 DYM			B21F	M&G	R
RH4	Dove	C504 DYM			B21F	M&G	R
RH5	Owl	C505 DYM			B21F	M&G	R
RH6	Swift	C506 DYM			B21F	M&G	R
RH7	Swallow	C507 DYM			B21F	M&G	R
RH8	Swan	C508 DYM			B21F	M&G	R
RH9	Heron	C509 DYM			B21F	M&G	R
RH10	Wren	C510 DYM			B21F	M&G	BB
RH11	Sparrow	C511 DYM			B21F	M&G	BB
RH12	Woodpecker	C512 DYM			B21F	M&G	BB
RH13	Blackbird	D513 FYL			B21F	M&G	BB; R
RH14	Nightingale	D514 FYL			B21F	EB	M&G; BB
RH15	Kingfisher	C515 DYM			B21F	M&G	BB; R
RH16	Lark	C516 DYM			B21F	M&G	BB
RH17	Snipe	C517 DYM			B21F	M&G	BB
RH18	Sandpiper	C518 DYM			B21F	M&G	BB
RH19	Canary *	D519 FYL			B21F	EB	M&G; CB; R
RH20	Teal	D520 FYL			B21F	EB	BB
RH21	Gannet	C521 DYM			B21F	M&G	BB
RH22	Jay *	D522 FYL			B21F	EB	CB; R
RH23	Hawk	C523 DYM			DP21F	M&G	BB
RI I24	Seagull	D524 FYL			DP21F	M&G	BB; R

* These names were allocated but never carried. After RH18 "Sandpiper" & RH23 "Hawk" departed
to Bexleybus, their names were reassigned to RH19 & RH22 respectively.

Permanent & semi-permanent vehicles - continued

FLEET NO.	NAME	REG. NO.	CHASSIS	BODY	SEATING LAYOUT	ORIGINAL LIVERY	LATER LIVERIES
OV1	Typhoon	C525 DYM	VW LT55	Optare	B25F	M&G	
OV2	Hurricane	C526DYT		City Pacer		M&G	R; M&G
OV3	Tornado	C527 DYT				M&G	
OV4	Chinook	C528DYT				M&G	
OV5	Whirlwind	D529 FYL				M&G	R
OV26		D358 JUM				R	
OV38		D370 JUM				R	
OV44		D376 JUM				R	
OV49		D381 JUM				R	
A1		NYN 1Y	Dodge	Rootes	B19F	R	
A2		NYN 2Y				R	
MRL 65		E641 KYW	Metrorider	MCW	B33F	M&G	R
MRL 66	Sparrow II	E642 KYW			B33F	M&G	R
MRL 67*	Blackbird II	E643 KYW			B33F	M&G	R
MRL 68*	Nightingale II	E644 KYW			B33F	M&G	R
MRL 69	Kingfisher II	E645 KYW			B33F	M&G	R
MRL 70	Seagull	E646 KYW			B33F	M&G	R
MRL 71	Snipe II	E647 KYW			B33F	M&G	R
MRL 72	Sandpiper II	E648 KYW			B33F	M&G	R
MRL 73	Teal II	E649 KYW			B33F	M&G	R
MRL 74	Gannet II	E650 KYW			DP33F	M&G	R
MRL 75	Woodpecker II	E705 LYU			DP33F	M&G	R
MRL 76		E706 LYU			DP33F	M&G	R
MRL 77*	Seagull II	F197 YDA			B33F	M&G	R

* The MRL class did not carry fleet numbers whilst in maroon & grey livery. However, three carried "M" numbers, being an unofficial system based on the last two numbers on the registration plate. MRL67 - M43; MRL68 - M44; MRL77 - M97.

After repaint into red, they joined the LBL MRL numbering sequence.

Permanent & semi-permanent vehicles - continued

FLEET NO.	NAME	REG. NO.	CHASSIS	BODY	SEATING LAYOUT	ORIGINAL LIVERY	LATER REG. NO.
DT 28	Pride of Carlyle	G28 TGW	Dennis Dart	Carlyle	DP28F	R	49 CLT
DT 29		G29 TGW			B28F	R	
DT 30		G30 TGW			DP28F	R	
DT 31		G31 TGW			DP28F	R	
DT 32		G32 TGW			B28F	R	VLT 240
DT 33		G33 TGW			B28F	R	
DT 34		G34 TGW			B28F	R	
DT 35		G35 TGW			B28F	R	
DT 36		G36 TGW			B28F	R	
DT 37		G37 TGW			B28F	R	
DT 38		G38 TGW			B28F	R	
DT 39		G39 TGW			B28F	R	
DT 40		G40 TGW			B28F	R	
DT 41		G41 TGW			B28F	R	
DT 55		G55 TGW			DP28F	R	WLT 575
MC 1		F430 BOP	Mercedes 811D	Carlyle	B28F	R	WLT 491 F286 KGK
MC2		H882 LOX			B28F	R	
MC3		H883 LOX			B28F	R	
MC4		H884 LOX			B28F	R	WLT 400 H509 AGC
MC5		H885 LOX			B28F	R	
FM1	Capricorn	K521 EFL	Iveco Daily 49-10	Marshall	B23F	R	
FM2	Aquarius	K522 EFL				R	
FM3	Pisces	K523 EFL				R	
FM4	Aries	K524 EFL				R	
FM5	Taurus	K525 EFL				R	
FM6	Gemini	K526 EFL				R	
FM7	Scorpio*	K527 EFL				R	
FM8	Leo	K528 EFL				R	
FM9	Virgo	K529 EFL				R	
FM10	Libra	K530 EFL				R	

* FM7 was originally named "Cancer" in Zodiac order, but was renamed "Scorpio" after a few days.

ROUNDABOUT FLEET LIST semi-permanent vehicles - continued

FLEET NO.	REG. NO.	CHASSIS	BODY	SEATING LAYOUT	ORIGINAL LIVERY
BL85	OJD 85R	Bristol LH6L	ECW	B39F	R&W
MT4	F394 DHL	Mercedes 709D	Reeve Burgess	B24F	R
MR14	D474 PON	MCW Metrorider	MCW	B23F	R

ROUNDABOUT FLEET LIST loans & demonstrators

FLEET NO.	REG. NO.	CHASSIS	BODY	LIVERY	ORIGIN
	C525 EWR	VW LT 55	Optare City pacer	silver	Optare demonstrator
	D113 TFT	Freight Rover Sherpa	Carlyle	white	Newcastle Busways
	D121 TFT	Freight Rover Sherpa	Carlyle	white	Newcastle Busways
	D262 OOJ	Freight Rover Sherpa	Carlyle	yellow & red	Manchester Minibuses
	D632 NOE	MCW Metrorider	MCW	blue & sliver	West Midlands Travel
	E629 AMA	Iveco	Carlyle	red	Carlyle demonstrator
	E76 TDA	MCW Metrorider	MCW	silver	MCW demonstrator
	E968 SVP	Freight Rover Sherpa	Carlyle	white	Carlyle demonstrator
	E630 MAC	Talbot	Talbot Pullman	white	Talbot demonstrator
MR25	E125 KYW	MCW Metrorider	MCW	red	Selkent float
	E127 KYW	MCW Metrorider	MCW	white / stripes	Stagecoach Newcastle
MR35	E135 KYW	MCW Metrorider	MCW	red	Selkent float
MR38	E138 KYW	MCW Metrorider	MCW	red	Selkent float
	E146 KYW	MCW Metrorider	MCW	white / stripes	Stagecoach Newcastle
MR49	E149 KYW	MCW Metrorider	MCW	red	Selkent float
MR51	E151 KYW	MCW Metrorider	MCW	red	Selkent float
BB29	E929 KYR	MCW Metrorider	MCW	blue / cream	Bexleybus
BB30	E930 KYR	MCW Metrorider	MCW	blue / cream	Bexleybus
BB31	E631 KYW	MCW Metrorider	MCW	blue / cream	Bexleybus
BB32	E632 KYW	MCW Metrorider	MCW	blue / cream	Bexleybus
BB33	E633 KYW	MCW Metrorider	MCW	blue / cream	Bexleybus
BB34	E634 KYW	MCW Metrorider	MCW	blue / cream	Bexleybus
BB35	E635 KYW	MCW Metrorider	MCW	blue / cream	Bexleybus
BB36	E636 KYW	MCW Metrorider	MCW	blue / cream	Bexleybus
BB37	E637 KYW	MCW Metrorider	MCW	blue / cream	Bexleybus
MRL118	F118 YVP	MCW Metrorider	MCW	red	LBL
	F419 BOP	Freight Rover Sherpa	Carlyle	yellow	Carlyle demonstrator
	F75 AKB	Renault	Northern Counties	cream & blue	Preston Bus

Roundabout Fleet List - loans & demonstrators continued

FLEET	REG. NO.	CHASSIS	BODY	LIVERY	ORIGIN
SR60	F160 FWY	Mercedes	Optare	red	LBL
SR63	F163 FWY	Mercedes	Optare	red	LBL
MA4	F604 XMS	Mercedes	Alexander	red	LBL
MA9	F609 XMS	Mercedes	Alexander	red	LBL
ME1	G395 OWB	Mercedes	Crystals	red	LBL
	G495 FFA	Mercedes	AMI	metallic turquoise	The Potteries
	G689 KNW	Optare Metrorider	Optare	silver	Optare demonstrator
	G895 XPX	Dennis Dart	Portsdown	red & cream	Wadham Stringer
DT45	G45 TGW	Dennis Dart	Carlyle	red	LBL
	H727 LOL	Mercedes	Carlyle	white	Carlyle demonstrator
MRL142	H142 UUA	Optare Metrorider	Optare	red	LBL
MRL143	H143 UUA	Optare Metrorider	Optare	red	LBL
MRL144	H144 UUA	Optare Metrorider	Optare	red	LBL
MRL145	H145 UUA	Optare Metrorider	Optare	red	LBL
DW59	JDZ 2359	Dennis Dart	Wright	red	LBL
	K165 FYG	Optare Metrorider	Optare	yellow & white	Newcastle Busways
	K166 FYG	Optare Metrorider	Optare	yellow & white	Newcastle Busways

DEMONSTRATING THE DEMONSTRATORS:

E629 AMA, an Iveco with the Carlyle body (designed for the Freight Rover Sherpa) was the first of a succession of demonstrator midibuses.
The three track blind should have read "R1"! 22nd July 1988.

This Mercedes unusually carried a a body by Europa of Doncaster, later known as "Crystals Conversions". These bodies were carried by the Mercedes vehicles Crystals later deployed on routes R2 & R7. The vehicle was given fleet no. ME1 during its short stay with LBL. 23rd June 1990
Both photos in Orpington High Street:
K. Gurney

167

Roundabout Route Histories

ROUTE R1 / R11 *Running Nos. OB1-13*

1986 16 Aug **Route R1 (only)** introduced daily. RH allocated.
Operation thus (route R1 displayed on all journeys):
M-Sa (eve excepted) two overlapping sections:
  (i) Queen Marys Hospital – Green Street Green
  (ii) Grovelands – Bromley Common (Crown)
Eve & Su: Queen Marys – Bromley Common (Crown) throughout.

REPLACES: Route 229 Foots Cray – Green Street Green;
Route 261 Bromley Common – Orpington.

1987 from Aug Progressive conversion RH > MRL.

1987 31 Oct Double run introduced via Orpington Hospital thus:
M-F 0830-2030, Sa 1330-2030, on journeys Queen Marys Hospital - Green Street Green, also on evening through journeys within timespan; Su 1330-2030.
Use of **Route R11** introduced, being displayed on all journeys via Orpington Hospital irrespective of origin / destination

1988 16 Jul **Routes R1 / R11**: Double run introduced via Foots Cray Tesco 0830–2030 M-Sa only.

1990 9 Jun **Route R1:** progressive conversion MRL > DT
Route R11: progressive conversion MRL > DT, but due grounding problems at junction of Orpington Hospital approach road with Sevenoaks Road, DT operated journeys unable to serve hospital.

1990 14 Jul **Route R11:** withdrawn from Orpington Hospital whilst roadworks implemented to avoid grounding.

1990 15 Aug **Route R11:** reinstated via Orpington Hospital on completion of roadworks

1991 26 Dec **Route R11:** Boxing Day special service Queen Marys Hospital – Bromley North Station.

1992 21 Nov **Routes R1 / R11:** Sa/Su morning service introduced via Orpington Hospital from 0830 to match M-F service. Route R1 journeys renumbered R11 as appropriate. Routeing via Tesco introduced on Su 1000-1600 during store trading hours.

1995 2 Dec	**Routes R1 / R11:** Contract awarded to Centrewest (Orpington Buses). DP allocated (initially) from Swanley Garage (SJ). Routes R1 and R11 assume independent operation: **Route R1:** becomes Grovelands – Bromley Common (omitting Orpington Hospital) daily; **Route R11:** becomes Queen Marys Hospital – Green Street Green (via Orpington Hospital) daily.

ROUTE R2   *Running Nos. OB21-22*

1986 16 Aug	New route introduced M-F only, evenings excepted. RH allocated. Orpington Station – Biggin Hill Valley. Ten journeys southbound; eleven journeys northbound; irregular headways 60-85 minutes; 125 minute gap early afternoon. Journeys run direct Orpington Station – Sevenoaks Road (both directions), except for four southbound inter-peak journeys, which run via Spur Road, Gravel Pit Way, Homefield Rise and High Street. *REPLACES: Route 858 over similar routeing.*
1987 31 Oct	Introduced Sa; seven round journeys, all conforming to M-F inter-peak routeing.
1989 21 Oct	Additional early morning journey added M-Sa ex-Biggin Hill Valley. Limited stop formally introduced on journeys from Orpington 1600-1900 M-F: no passengers set down before Farnborough Hill / Shire Lane.
1992 21 Nov	Extended 0900-1700 Orpington Station via route R3 to Poverest Road, thence via Austin Road, Sidmouth Road, Amherst Drive, Dorney Rise, Sherborne Road, Church Hill Wood, Poverest Road, thence via route R3 to Petts Wood Station. Southbound journeys operating via Spur Road, Gravel Pit Way, Homefield Rise and High Street **continue** to observe this routeing, thus serving Orpington Memorial (Mc Donalds) twice. Clockface hourly timetable introduced for most of day.
1993 May	Progressive conversion RH > FM.
1993 14 Aug	Rerouted in St Mary Cray: buses run entire length of Amherst Drive, thence via Sefton Road, Sherborne Road (omitting Dorney Rise), to line of route. Southbound routeing via Spur Road,etc. withdrawn.
1995 2 Dec	Contract awarded to Crystals. Mercedes midibus allocated from Dartford premises.

ROUTE R3   *Running Nos. OB31-34*

1986 16 Aug
.

New route introduced M-Sa; OV allocated.

Petts Wood Station – Poverest Road – Kent Road – Lower Road – Orpington – Repton Road – Eton Road – The Highway – Chelsfield Station. Extended, evenings excepted, via Windsor Drive - Vine Road - Worlds End Lane – Green Street Green (Rose & Crown).

Double running Orpington Memorial – Orpington Station as follows:
M-F morning peak northbound journeys only;
M-F afternoon peak southbound journeys only;
M-Sa evenings journeys in both directions.

SaO last departure 2240 ex-Petts Wood extended from Chelsfield Station via daytime routeing to Green Street Green, thence uniquely via Cudham – Knockholt Pound – Halstead – Watercroft Road – Court Road (throughout) – Carlton Parade.

REPLACES: Route 284 ("experimental" since 14 May 1984, withdrawn after 15 Aug 1986) M-F Petts Wood Station – Poverest Road – Cray Avenue – Orpington Station.

REPLACES: Route 493 Chelsfield Station – Green Street Green (confined to Orpington - Ramsden after 15 Aug 1986).

1989 21 Oct

M-F early morning ex-OB garage positioning journeys livened-up Kent Road / Cray Avenue – Petts Wood Station to provide earlier connections with trains.

M-Sa single late night OB garage journey ex-R1 run in service as R3 0012 ex-Petts Wood – Kent Road / Cray Avenue to meet late night train.

1990 Aug

Progressive conversion OV > MC.

1992 21 Nov

Rerouted in Green Street Green to form a live one-way loop incorporating 2 min stand time at Queens Head: from Windsor Drive diverted via Glentrammon Road – High Street – Worlds End Lane – Vine Road – Windsor Drive thence as existing line of route.

All journeys extended beyond Chelsfield Station.

All journeys operate via Orpington Station.

0012 ex-Petts Wood retarded to 0030, subsequently to 0037.

170

1995 2 Dec   Contract awarded to Centrewest (Orpington Buses). Allocated (initially) from SJ. Intended MM class awaiting commissioning at Marshalls. Operated by MA and DP for time being.

Su service introduced.

SaO late night journey to Cudham, etc. withdrawn beyond Green Street Green.

ROUTE R4   *Running Nos. OB41-44*

1986 16 Aug   New route introduced M-Sa evenings excepted; RH allocated. Half-hourly headway.
Locks Bottom (Pallant Way) – Crofton Road – Starts Hill Road – Farnborough by-Pass – Tubbenden Lane – Station Road – Orpington High Street – Lower Road – St Mary Cray High Street – Main Road – Chalk Pit Avenue – Pauls Cray Hill (Augustine Road).

Operates via Orpington Station in Pauls Cray Hill direction only.

1987 31 Oct   Headway improved to 20 minutes.

1989 12 Jun   Due long-term roadworks in Tubbenden Lane, diverted via Southcroft Road, Ridgeway Crescent, Leamington Avenue, Borkwood Way, Northlands Avenue, Oakleigh Gardens, Sevenoaks Road, Farnborough Hill, Farnborough by-Pass, Starts Hill Road.

1989 Dec   Further diverted due roadworks Station Road, Sevenoaks Way, Main Road. 20 minute headway unable to be maintained; emergency timetable introduced at half-hourly headway.

1991 27 Apr   Due popular demand, routeing off Tubbenden Lane permanently adopted thus: Tubbenden Drive – Northlands Avenue –Southlands Avenue – Beechcroft Lane. 20 minute headway reintroduced.

1992 21 Nov   Additional SDO journeys introduced:
0803 ex-Pauls Cray Hill; 1603 ex-Locks Bottom.

1993 May   Progressive conversion RH > FM

1995 2 Dec   Contract awarded to Centrewest (Orpington Buses). Allocated (initially) from SJ. Intended MM class awaiting commissioning at Marshalls. Operated by MA and DP for time being.

Su service introduced from midday.
Evening service introduced daily.
Operates via Orpington Station in both directions.

ROUTE R5   *Running No. OB25*

1986 16 Aug   New route introduced M-Sa (evenings excepted).

REPLACES: Route 471.

Single RH allocated.
Additional M-F peak period single Leyland National (LS) allocated from TB.

RH deployed all day on circular routeing, originating from Orpington Station hourly either:

    (i)   Orpington Station – Green Street Green – Pratts Bottom – Knockholt Pound – Cudham – Green Street Green – Orpington Station (clockwise); or:

    (ii) Orpington Station – Green Street Green – Cudham – Knockholt Pound – Pratts Bottom - Green Street Green – Orpington Station (anti-clockwise).

During M-F morning peak, clockwise routeing adopted.

During M-F afternoon peak, anti-clockwise routeing adopted.

Between M-F peaks and all day Sa, journeys alternate clockwise / anti-clockwise, and operate via Spur Rd, Gravel Pit Way, Orpington High Street.

In M-F peaks, LS deployed to maintain a service over the Orpington – Pratts Bottom – Knockholt Pound leg in the opposite direction to the RH, and support route R6 in the Halstead / Badgers Mount area. Three morning and four afternoon journeys, mostly circular.

1988 16 Jul   Peak period LS operation replaced by additional RH/OV allocated from OB. Between 1555 and 1805 passengers not carried locally between Orpington Station and Green Street Green High Street on all journeys.

Use of route number 471 reinstated to support R5 M-F with-flow peaks Green Street Green – Orpington Station. Single LS allocated from TB: operating as follows:

Ex-Green Street Green 0648 – 0848 20 minute headway;
Ex-Orpington Station 1630 - 1850 20 minute headway. Journeys operate via Spur Road, Gravel Pit Way, Orpington High Street.

1992 21 Nov   Double run Knockholt Pound – Halstead introduced on all journeys. The additional peak period RH allocation (performing journeys via Badgers Mount) transferred to reinstated companion route R6.

471 withdrawn. Replaced by route 358, revamped to start at Orpington station (instead of Orpington Walnuts) and run via Green Street Green (instead of Crofton Road).

1993 4 Dec   Contract awarded to Kentish Bus Metrorider allocated from Dunton Green Garage (DG) (pending delivery of two Dormobile bodied Iveco midibuses ordered for routes R5 & R6).

<u>ROUTE R6</u>   *Running No. OB26*

1986 16 Aug   New route introduced M-Sa, evenings excepted. OV allocated.

Principal routeing:
Orpington Station – Sevenoaks Road – Warren Road – Chelsfield Station – The Highway – Chelsfield Village – Badgers Mount – Halstead – Knockholt Pound – Dunton Green – Riverhead – Sevenoaks.

Four return journeys, plus several Mon-Fri peak and SDO short workings

REPLACES: 431 Court Road –Sevenoaks (withdrawn after 15 Aug)

REPLACES: 493 Orpington Station – Chelsfield Station (confined to Orpington – Ramsden after 15 Aug)

1987 30 May   Withdrawn Halstead – Sevenoaks. Replaced over this sector by new Kentish Bus route 22 Bromley – Green Street Green – Pratts Bottom – Badgers Mount – Halstead – Knockholt Pound – Dunton Green – Riverhead – Sevenoaks – Tonbridge – Tunbridge Wells.

(KB 22 replaced Green Line 706 withdrawn after 29 May 1987. New KB route 21 introduced 30 May 1987: two return journeys M-Sa Orpington Walnuts – Spur Road – Court Road – Polhill – Sevenoaks.)

1988 26 Mar   Withdrawn entirely. Replaced by Kentish Bus routes 17 & 18.

(KB 17 {formerly 477} had been introduced 16 Jan 1988 M-Sa {half-hourly} Joyce Green – Dartford – Hextable – Swanley – Orpington – Spur Road – Court Road – Chelsfield Village – Badgers Mount – Halstead – Knockholt Pound – Dunton Green – Riverhead – Sevenoaks.)

(From 26 Mar 1988, half of KB 17 renumbered 18 running via KB 17 to Court Road thence via Chelsfield Village – Badgers Mount – Polhill – Dunton Green – Riverhead – Bat & Ball – Sevenoaks.)

1992 21 Nov	Use of route number reinstated to distinguish the route R5 M-F peak period journeys via Badgers Mount. All journeys circular either:

(i) Orpington Station – Green Street Green – Pratts Bottom – Badgers Mount – Halstead – Knockholt Pound – Pratts Bottom – Green Street Green – Orpington Station (clockwise); two morning peak and two afternoon peak journets.

(ii) Orpington Station – Green Street Green - Pratts Bottom – Knockholt Pound – Halstead - Badgers Mount – Pratts Bottom – Green Street Green – Orpington Station (anti-clockwise); one morning peak and two afternoon peaks journeys.

1993 6 Sep All afternoon peak journeys revised to operate anti-clockwise; Additional evening peak journey added Orpington Station – Halstead.

1993 4 Dec Contract awarded to Kentish Bus Metrorider allocated from DG.

ROUTE R7 *Running No. OB27*

1988 16 Jul New route introduced M-Sa 0900-1700 hourly. Cockmannings estate – St Mary Cray – Orpington – Knoll – Petts Wood – Coppice estate loop – Petts Wood – Knoll – Orpington – St Mary Cray – Cockmannings estate.

OV allocated from OB (trading as Roundabout), using a single vehicle advertised as "freed up due to the withdrawal of route R6, and in response to requests for a bus service to the Cockmannings and Coppice estates". In practice often worked by RH.

Route via: Waldenhurst Road (new stand), Cockmannings Road, Chelsfield Road, Kent Road, Lower Road, Orpington High Street, circuit of Orpington Memorial, Orpington High Street, Knoll Rise, Mayfield Avenue, Chislehurst Road, Crofton Lane, St Johns Road, Tudor Way, Queensway (Petts Wood Station), Franks Wood Avenue, Oxhawth Crescent, Farringdon Avenue, Almond Way, Whitebeam Avenue, Lovelace Avenue, Ash Row, Larch Way, Farringdon Avenue, Oxhawth Crescent, Franks Wood Avenue, Queensway (Petts Wood Station), Tudor Way, St Johns Road, Crofton Lane, Chislehurst Road, Mayfield Avenue, Knoll Rise, left turn direct Orpington High Street, Lower Road, Kent Road, Chelsfield Road, Rookesley Road, Somerden Road, Waldenhurst Road.

1989 23 Oct   The single allocated vehicle becomes further deployed M-F peak hours to provide 20 minute headway Petts Wood Station, West Approach – Coppice estate loop – Petts Wood Station, West Approach.

1991 29 Sep   Closure of Knoll Rise to through traffic for eight weeks. Diverted from Knoll Rise via Lucerne Road, St Kilda Road, Beswick Road, Broomhill Road / White Hart Road.

1992 21 Nov   Contract awarded to Kentish Bus. Metrorider allocated from Dartford Garage (DT). Route entirely revamped:

M-Sa, evenings excepted, 20 minute headway: Petts Wood Station – Coppice – Knoll – Orpington High Street – Orpington Station – St Mary Cray Village – St Mary Cray estates. One bus per hour extended via route 477 to/from Dartford.

M-Sa evenings hourly: Orpington Station – St Mary Cray Estates – Dartford. Between St Mary Cray Estates and Dartford, route number R76 displayed and journeys operate via Joydens Wood instead of Hextable.

Su hourly from mid-morning: Orpington Station – St Mary Cray Estates – Dartford. Between St Mary Cray Estates and Dartford alternate journeys display route number R76 and operate via Joydens Wood instead of Hextable.

REPLACES: routes 476 / 477 / 478 Orpington – Crockenhill.

ABANDONED: St Mary Cray – Cockmannings (covered by new route R8)

Route via: West Approach (Petts Wood Station), Franks Wood Avenue, Oxhawth Crescent, Farringdon Avenue, Almond Way, Whitebeam Avenue, Lovelace Avenue (throughout), Oxhawth Crescent, Chesham Avenue, Woodhurst Avenue, Nightingale Road, Shepperton Road, Towncourt Lane, Tudor Way, St Johns Road, Crofton Lane, Chislehurst Road, Mayfield Avenue, Knoll Rise, Orpington High Street, Orpington Station, Orpington High Street, Lower Road, Kent Road, St Mary Cray High Street, Millbrook Road, Sandway Road, Wooton Green, Sweeps Lane, Blacksmiths Lane, Burrfield Drive, Crockenhill Road, Sweeps Lane, thence returning to Petts Wood via outward routeing.

ROUTE R8   *Running No. OB28*

1992 21 Nov   New route Cockmannings estate – St Mary Cray – Orpington – Charterhouse Road – Chelsfield village loop – Charterhouse Road - Orpington – St Mary Cray – Cockmannings estate.

M-F 0800-1900 plus short journey 0656 ex-Chelsfield to Orpington Station Sa 0800-1800.

RH allocated.

Route via: Waldenhurst Road, Cockmannings Road, Chelsfield Road, Kent Road, Lower Road, Orpington High Street, double run Orpington Station, Sevenoaks Road, Charterhouse Road, Court Road, Warren Road, Bucks Cross Road, Maypole Road, Shoreham Lane, Hewitts Road, Court Road, Charterhouse Road, Sevenoaks Road, double run Orpington Station, Orpington High Street, Lower Road, Kent Road, Chelsfield Road, Rookesley Road (throughout), Renton Drive, Waldenhurst Road.

REPLACES: routes 476/477/478 Orpington Memorial – Chelsfield but via Sevenoaks Road and Charterhouse Road instead of Spur Road and part of Court Road.

REPLACES: route R7 St Mary Cray – Cockmannings estate, but with different routeing within estate.

1993 May   Progressive conversion RH > FM.

1994   Regularly allocated to BL85 and later MT4.

1995 2 Nov   Contract awarded to LondonLinks. Metrorider allocated from Kentish Bus' Dunton Green Garage (DG).

Where Are They Now?

The Survivors (in Spring 2010)

<u>RH</u>

RH1 'Kestrel' - Preservationist, Orpington (pending restoration)
RH16 'Lark' – F. Wooley Coaches, Llanedwin, Anglesey, Wales

<u>OV</u>

OV2 'Hurricane' - London Transport Museum, Acton (preserved)
OV3 'Tornado' - Unknown owner, Whitley Bay (campervan non-PSV)

<u>MRL</u>

MRL69 'Kingfisher II' - St Malachy's College, Belfast, Northern Ireland

<u>DW</u>

DW59 - S & B Training College, Bristol, Avon (likely to be in pieces)

<u>DT</u>

DT29 - County Coaches, Canterbury, Kent
DT32 - Lowger Bus Lines, St Johns, Antigua
DT34 - Sunrise Travel, West Bromwich, West Midlands
DT37 - Travel Express, Wolverhampton, West Midlands
DT39 - Emsworth & District, Southbourne

<u>FM</u>

FM1 'Capricorn' - Ross's Minibuses, Struy, Inverness, Highlands
FM2 'Aquarius' - Irvings, Dalton, Carlisle, Cumbria
FM3 'Pisces' - Moreton Coach Hire, Moreton, Derby, Derbyshire
FM4 'Aries' - VG Coaches, Crewe, Cheshire
FM6 'Gemini' - Coach House Travel, Dorchester

The time: 00.50; the date: Saturday 2nd December 1995; the place: Unit 5, Nugent Industrial Estate; the sad occasion: conclusion of the Roundabout operation, as RH1 "Kestrel" comes home for the last time. *Photo: Andrew Jeffreys*

The Home

So what became of OB? In 2005, Nugent Industrial Estate was bulldozed to the ground, and a new shopping centre created. The site soon established itself as the Nugent Retail Park, attracting many high profile High Street names to locate there: plush, modern shops and cafes replacing the drab factory-style warehousing. Debenhams now stands on the site occupied by unit 17, whilst the large car parking area fronting Clarkes Shoes covers the land where unit 5 stood.

DEMOLITION IN PROGRESS - THE END: 2005. *Photo: Paul Bishop*

Epilogue by the Author

Without question, the success of *Roundabout* paved the way to what is today's extensive network of bus services in Orpington. By fulfilling the basic fundamentals of good bus operating practice, a clear and reputable business model evolved. A great base of experience flowed from the pioneering results of the Roundabout project. Many localised networks developed all over the suburbs and in central London also: "B" Bexleyheath; "H" Harrow; "P" Peckham"; "W" Walthamstow, to name but a few. The little buses of Orpington with their charismatic charm had created a "personal" touch second to none. Yet after nine years' reputable operation, Roundabout was "seen off" by an aggressive bid all in the name of competitive tendering, for "bottom line cost" was the culture LRT appeared to adopt. Privatisation had opened up the opportunity for other operators to innovate, but events by the end of the millennium, notably the demise of certain "low cost" operators in southeast London, stunned LRT into acknowledging proven ability before awarding contracts, but that was too late for Roundabout. How closely Stagecoach Selkent lost out on costings in the 1995 round of tenders, we shall probably never know.

Thankfully some effort has been made to preserve part of the maroon and grey culture of Roundabout's heritage, by way of the pristine example of the Optare City Pacer OV2 *"Hurricane"* at the LT Museum collection, Acton.

Back in 2004, I made enquiries into preservation of an RH vehicle, and managed to trace RH5 *"Owl"* with an operator in Cumbria - sadly further communication was not forthcoming and RH5 ended up at PVS Barnsley. However soon after this, I became instrumental in the transfer into safe keeping of RH1 *"Kestrel"*. She was laid up in an open yard notorious for vandalism in North Kent looking somewhat forlorn and was serving as a home to a feral cat and her kittens - the seats were caked with fur! I made enquiries into the ownership and to ascertain any future intentions for the vehicle, and managed to secure a new home and owner for the bus. RH1 duly started on the key with just a simple battery boost, and was driven to her new home where she is pending full restoration.

Without forgetting the Roundabout red bus years, I made a quest to see if an FM could be saved, and after many talks with an operator in Scotland, it became clear that FM1 *"Capricorn"* – the bus I named some years ago- could be made available to a keen bus preservationist! Any takers?!

As one chapter closed another opened for DT32! After leaving OB a month earlier, she remained local as a servant on the B99 contract at TB. Seen here boarding "park & riders" in Elmfield Road, Bromley, December 1995, DT32 is being overtaken by the fresh-faced victor carrying the title "Orpington Buses" – a new Volvo on route 61. Perhaps this closing scene tells us it is time to bow our heads respectfully, and concede that the Roundabout story is well and truly told and consigned to the history books.

RH1 in June 2010 undergoing restoration

Copyright Tom Gurney

TOM GURNEY
Petts Wood
www.redbuspublishing.co.uk